SAMUEL BECKETT

A Study of the Short Fiction

Also available in Twayne's Studies in Short Fiction Series

Twayne's Studies in Short Fiction

Gordon Weaver, General Editor
Oklahoma State University

SAMUEL BECKETT

—— A Study of the Short Fiction ——

Robert Cochran
University of Arkansas

TWAYNE PUBLISHERS • NEW YORK
Maxwell Macmillan Canada • Toronto
Maxwell Macmillan International • New York Oxford Singapore Sydney

Twayne's Studies in Short Fiction Series, No. 29

Twayne Publishers
Macmillan Publishing Company
866 Third Avenue
New York, NY 10022

Maxwell Macmillan Canada, Inc.
1200 Eglinton Avenue East
Suite 200
Don Mills, Ontario M3C 3N1

Macmillan Publishing Company is part of the Maxwell Communication Group of Companies.

Library of Congress Cataloging-in-Publication Data

Cochran, Robert, 1943–
    Samuel Beckett: a study of the short fiction / Robert Cochran.
        p.   cm.—(Twayne's studies in short fiction series; no. 29)
    Includes bibliographical references and index.
    ISBN 0-8057-8320-2
    1. Beckett, Samuel, 1906–1989—Fictional works.   2. Short story.
I. Title.   II. Series: Twayne's studies in short fiction; no. 29.
PR6003.E282Z594   1991
823'.912—dc20
                                                                    91-26298
                                                                    CIP

The paper used in this publication meets the minimum requirements of American National Standard for Information Sciences—Permanence of Paper for Printed Library Materials. ANSI Z3948-1984.

10 9 8 7 6 5 4 3 2 1

Printed in the United States of America.

For Suzanne

Contents

Preface

Samuel Beckett has been famous in the world of letters for nearly 40 years, but remains even now best known for his plays and novels. A study that concentrates on his short fiction, therefore, except as a work addressed to specialists, must solicit its readership on grounds other than fashion, and must in fact seem inescapably perverse, in company with studies such as *Chekhov's Medical Practice* or *Shakespeare the Glover*. But here a little perversity may be all to the good—the stories, unburdened by the famous career of the plays and novels, may better advance their own more essentially literary merits. The description of such virtues will occupy a major place in this study.

What is more, it happens that the stories serve admirably as introductions to Beckett's other works. Although defense of this proposition will occupy only a minor place in this study, it may be noted that Beckett published stories before he published novels or plays, that he struggled through what appears in retrospect to be a period of artistic crisis in the 1960s by managing to write stories while remaining unable to write plays or novels, and that even later, after the somewhat ampler successes of the 1970s, which also included stories, his final works, those of the 1980s, are dominated by short fiction.

Samuel Beckett, then, produced short fiction throughout his writing life, and the relationship between his efforts in short fiction and those in other genres is intimate and interdependent. Two stories from his first collection, *More Pricks than Kicks*, were first written as parts of the early, unpublished novel *Dream of Fair to Middling Women*. A story entitled "Echo's Bones" was originally intended as the finale of *More Pricks than Kicks;* it was excised at an editor's insistence, but a poem of the same title appeared the following year, lending its title to *Echo's Bones and Other Precipitates*. The thirteen brief works in *Texts for Nothing*, published in 1950, have been understood as developing directly from the impasse that ended *The Unnamable* in 1949. That novel, the last in the *Three Novels* trilogy, ends with a mixing of voices and the paradoxical juxtaposition of recognized inability and asserted competence: "I don't know, I'll never know, in the silence you don't know, you must go on, I can't go on, I'll go on."[1] The first of the *Texts* continues in just this vein: "Suddenly, no, at last, long last I couldn't any more, I couldn't go on."[2]

The point needs no belaboring here; it will be thoroughly pummeled in the treatment of individual stories, where recourse to novels, plays, and poems will be frequent. It is all one work, finally, written by one man possessed by, in sure dispossession of, one world. In fact, a thread that it is hoped will help bind this study into a coherent, seamless whole, or failing this at least keep it from flying asunder altogether, will be the philistine notion that what is offered in Beckett's work is at bottom considerably less arcane and difficult to approach than would be suggested by the formidable erudition displayed in its explication by professional appreciators.

The author himself, in one of his most obscure works, can be cited in support of such a common thought. In 1945, in *Cahiers d'art*, Beckett published an appreciation of the painters Bram and Geer van Velde that at several points descends to general remarks concerning aesthetics and criticism. At one point a hypothetical member of the artist's public is introduced, an "inoffensif loufoque qui court, comme d'autres au cinéma, dans les galeries, au musée et jusque dans les églises avec l'espoir—tenez-vous bien—de jouir. Il ne veut pas s'instruire, le cochon, ni devenir meilleur. Il ne pense qu'à son plaisir" (a harmless loony who, as others go to movies, haunts galleries and museums, and sometimes even churches in the hope, note this, of pleasure. He does not want to learn, the pig, or become better. He thinks only of his own pleasure).[3]

But what of this slob, this insult to the galleries, many of them maintained at public expense or, what is worse, private subscription? Beckett could not be more emphatic: "C'est lui qui justifie l'existence de la peinture en tant que chose publique" (349; It is he who justifies the public existence of painting). This is a surprising sentiment, surprisingly expressed, from an author famed for his own formidable learning and for the obscurity and inaccessibility of his work. But it is in fact recurrent. *How It Is*, in the bleak welter of its crawling sufferers, includes one bald narrator's assertion: "another image yet another a boy sitting on a bed in the dark or a small old man I can't see with his head be it young or be it old his head in his hands I appropriate that heart."[4] This last element is a syntactic afterthought, hanging like a run-on tail at the end. It is easy to miss; so is the center of a target. *Watt*, produced 15 years earlier, broached the very theme in the interrogative, for potential future appropriation, in the "Addenda" consigned by "fatigue and disgust" to the back of the book but commended nonetheless as "precious and illuminating," worthy of being "carefully studied" by the reader:

> who may tell the tale
> of the old man?
> weigh absence in a scale
> mete want with a span?[5]

Beckett's fabled obscurity, again and again, emerges as only a part of the comedy, only a part of the tragedy. It is one thing for an author to be well read and quite another for him to require that reading of his audience. This author does not. The critic, offering himself as a useful guide to the uninitiated, should hesitate, perhaps, to offer his considerable ignorance as an important credential, to present himself as the "inoffensif loufoque" embodied as if this were a claim in his favor. But one could do worse. The American writer William Gass, himself an impressively learned philosophy professor and author of postmodern fictions, once described himself and his practice in terms that are helpful for approaching Beckett: "I'm a romantic basically; desperately trying to overcome it by rushing after formal procedures all over the place." The "formal procedures," Gass goes on to make clear, are protective devices, raised against what are perceived as personal weaknesses: "I really feel I'm liable to go off in twelve different directions if I'm not very, very careful. It's just sick. I'm just soppy."[6]

Romantic? Samuel Beckett? The term is too large, perhaps, too loaded with varied and even contradictory meanings. But one could do worse. Consider the eponymous hero of *Krapp's Last Tape*, musing in his "den," recording his assessment of another year. At one point he tells himself to give it up: "Ah finish your booze now and get to your bed. Go on with this drivel in the morning. Or leave it at that. (*Pause.*) Leave it at that."[7] The tone is harsh, full of self-contempt. But this is not the end. He does not leave it at that, cannot leave it at that. After another pause, he continues in a very different vein: "Lie propped up in the dark—and wander. Be again in the dingle on a Christmas Eve, gathering holly, the red-berried. (*Pause.*) Be again on Croghan on a Sunday morning, in the haze, with the bitch, stop and listen to the bells" (*KLT*, 26). A new tone, unabashedly lyric, has intervened, despite the preceding imperatives to the contrary.

A similar affirmation, this time made by Beckett in his own voice, appears in a 1934 review, where German poet and poseur Rainer Maria Rilke is scolded for "petulance" and his poem "Der Einsame," with its patronizing tone ("I move among these human vegetables. . . . But my horizon's full of phantasy"), is attacked for its snobbery. Rilke, in his young critic's leveling eye, is "a child who cannot pause to learn, as Heine learned, the fantasy investing 'human vegetables.'"[8] Beckett himself, even in the earliest, most aggressively learned works, never lost sight of this fantasy.

His first collection of stories, for example, the 1934 *More Pricks than Kicks*, brings on stage for a moment "a complete down-and-out," a tinker camped by the roadside with his cart. The action is simple: Belacqua Shuah, the shabby hero of the stories, is out for a walk with his dog, a Kerry Blue bitch. They meet the tinker, the bitch first sniffs, then urinates on the tinker's ragged trousers, and the tinker reacts to this insult. "Wettin me throusers," he says, "Wuss 'n meself."[9] This comment is delivered, the narrative stresses, "mildly," in a voice "devoid of rancour," and when Belacqua wishes the tinker good evening, praising at the same time the glorious weather, the "vagabond" responds magnificently: "A smile proof against all adversity transformed the sad face of the man under the cart. He was most handsome with his thick, if unkempt, black hair and moustache" (*MPTK*, 104). The passage concludes in unabashed lyricism: "The instinctive nobility of this splendid creature . . . disarmed all the pothooks and hangers of civility. Belacqua made an inarticulate flourish with his stick and passed down the road out of the life of this tinker, this real man at last" (*MPTK*, 104).

Such lyricism is much abashed but never suppressed in subsequent works. The heart, appropriately, will be an internal organ, worn far from the sleeve. But it will be pumping. It is important to keep this in mind, since Beckett's works have often struck readers and reviewers as cruel, cold, despairing. Critics and scholars, avid of a more imposing vocabulary, have found his works nihilistic, absurd, solipsistic. But this notion is mistaken in either wording—compassionate would be a better term, a murmured refusal of nihilism and cruelty, its restraint a rejection not of sentiment but of sentimentalism. Just as the slob in the gallery was offered as art's essential public, more crucial than the connoisseur, compassion, carefully distinguished from pity, will be the thematic key of keys for this polymath's deep reader. Even the apparent

cruelties themselves, carefully examined, are often either different
than they seem or serve as forms of self-defense directed against various pomposities and aggressions.

Consider, for example, the sad end of Lady Pedal at the close of
Malone Dies. This worthy—apparently a fiction within the fiction, a
character of the character Malone, but this does not matter in the
slightest to the reader caught up in their toils—is leading a company
of lunatics on an excursion. Her motive is charity, none more selfish:
"she was well off and lived for doing good and bringing a little happiness into the lives of those less fortunate than herself" (*TN*, 280). On
the trip itself, she urges her charges to give rein to their joy: "Sing!
Make the most of this glorious day! Banish your cares, for an hour or
so!" (*TN*, 285). In short, she is insufferable. Nobody, least of all readers
who have ever themselves been vulnerable to remotely analogous elee-
mosynary assaults, is sorry to see her fall and perhaps break her hip. It
is a learning experience, however belated, and may cure her meddling,
to the considerable relief of the bedlamites who are her victims. It is
comforting to hear her, in her final appearance, "moan and groan, as if
she were the only being on the face of the earth deserving of pity"
(*TN*, 287).

Samuel Beckett's art, and specifically his short fiction, will be presented here, then, as accessible and even primarily addressed to readers at great remove from centers of academic and artistic fashion. His
great learning will be understood as serving to demonstrate learning's
irrelevance; his famed pessimism will be seen as the sad face of the
clown; his stringent parings and reductions will be approached less as
deliberate formal innovations undertaken for their own sake or for their
calculated appeal to a weary cognoscenti than as restraints on himself,
on his own inability, shared with his creature Belacqua, to "resist a
lachrymose philosopher" (*MPTK*, 163). The artist in Beckett, an imperious skeptic perfectionist, maturing from erudition, distrusting the
seductions of lyric style, attempted a statement shorn of ornament, and
managed, year after year, book after book, subdued epics of persistence, masterful confessions of inadequacy, "the little murmur of un-
consenting man" (*TN*, 325).

This, as preliminary matter, "precious and illuminating material"
(*W*, 247), should be more than sufficient. Enough. It is time to abandon
this preface. On.

Notes

1. *Malone Dies, Molloy,* and *The Unnamable* appear in *Three Novels by Samuel Beckett* (New York: Grove Press, 1965), 414; hereafter cited in the text as *TN.*

2. *Stories and Texts for Nothing* (New York: Grove Press, 1967), 75.

3. "La Peinture des van Velde, ou: le monde et le pantalon," *Cahiers d'Art* 20–21 (1945–46): 349 (my translation); hereafter cited in the text.

4. *How It Is* (New York: Grove Press, 1964), 18.

5. *Watt* (New York: Grove Press, 1959), 247; hereafter cited in the text as *W.*

6. David Ohle, "William H. Gass Interview," *Cottonwood Review* (Spring 1969): 56.

7. *Krapp's Last Tape and Other Dramatic Pieces* (New York: Grove Press, 1960), 26; hereafter cited in the text as *KLT.*

8. Untitled review of *Poems* by Rainer Maria Rilke, as translated by J. B. Leishman, *Criterion* 13 (1934): 705, 706.

9. *More Pricks than Kicks* (New York: Grove Press, 1972), 103; hereafter cited in the text as *MPTK.*

Acknowledgments

Quotations from Samuel Beckett's work and letters copyright © by Grove Weidenfeld. Reprinted by permission.

Drawing of Samuel Beckett by Martha Olson. Printed by permission.

Excerpts from "Learning to Live with Death: 'Echo's Bones'" by Rubin Rabinovitz, *The Development of Samuel Beckett's Fiction.* © 1984 by the Board of Trustees of the University of Illinois. Reprinted by permission of the author and University of Illinois Press.

Excerpts from "Extorting Love's Tales From the Banished Son: Origins of Narratability in Samuel Beckett's 'First Love,'" by S. Jean Walton. © 1988 by The University of Wisconsin Press. Reprinted by permission.

Excerpts from "A Reading of Beckett's *Imagination Dead Imagine* by Brian Finney. © 1971 by Hofstra University Press. Reprinted by permission.

Excerpt from "The Structuring of Lessness" by Rosemary Pountney. © 1987 by *The Review of Contemporary Fiction.* Reprinted by permission.

Excerpts from "'Company': the mirror of Beckettian mimesis" by Eric P. Levy. © 1982 by *Journal of Beckett Studies.* Reprinted by permission.

Excerpts from "A Note on *Ill Seen Ill Said*" by Michael O'Brien. © 1987 by *The Review of Contemporary Fiction.* Reprinted by permission.

Excerpts from *Samuel Beckett: Poet and Critic, 1929–1949* by Lawrence E. Harvey. © 1970 by Princeton University Press. Reprinted by permission.

Excerpts from "Beckett and 'Merlin'" by Richard Seaver. © 1986 by Grove Press. Reprinted by permission.

Excerpts from *Samuel Beckett* by Dierdre Bair. © 1978 by Dierdre Bair. Reprinted by permission of Summit Books, a division of Simon and Schuster.

Excerpts from *Keaton: The Man Who Wouldn't Lie Down* by Tom Dardis. © 1979 by Thomas A. Dardis. Reprinted by permission.

Acknowledgments

Excerpts from *Giacometti* by James Lord. Copyright © 1965, 1980 by James Lord. Reprinted by permission of Farrar, Straus and Giroux, Inc.

Excerpts from "Beckett by the Madeleine" by Tom F. Driver. Reprinted by permission of Tom F. Driver.

"Beckett the Magnificant" by Madeleine Renaud, from *Beckett at Sixty: A Festschrift.* Copyright © 1966 by John Calder (Publishers) Ltd. Reprinted by permission of John Calder (Publishers)/Riverrun Press.

Part 1

THE SHORT FICTION

Beginnings

"Assumption"

Samuel Beckett was 23, a scholar in the making recently arrived in Paris as *lecteur* at the Ecole Normale Supérieure, when his first published study appeared in the spring of 1929. An auspicious debut, it was the lead essay in the imposingly titled *Our Exagmination Round His Factification for Incamination of Work in Progress*, a collection of essays in promotion and defense of what became *Finnegans Wake*. The young Beckett's work was titled "Dante . . . Bruno . Vico . . Joyce," and it was soon printed separately in the literary journal *transition*, along with another effort by the author. This other was no learned article, however, but a short story. Titled "Assumption," it was brief, running only four pages in print, and riddled with typos. It opened as in retrospect it needed to open, as if art imitated criticism, in brazen contradiction: "He could have shouted and could not."[1] Later, in more famous formulations, this trick will seem a badge of the author's presence, so much so that one instance will be a title, *Imagination Dead Imagine*, and a sampler of his work will utilize another, *I Can't Go On I'll Go On*, for its title.

"Assumption" centers its attention on a doomed figure, an adept of silence who is "partly artist" (269) by virtue of his "remarkable faculty of whispering the turmoil down" (268), but who is also, and fatally, partly man by virtue of a "wild rebellious surge that aspired violently toward realization in sound" (269). The most rigorous self-control has been necessary, and a terrible price has been exacted: "He felt he was losing, playing into the hands of the enemy by the very severity of his restrictions" (269–70). Not only will the unruly urge not subside—"He felt its implacable caged resentment, its longing to be released"—he is not even sure he wants it to: "he felt compassion as well as fear; he dreaded lest his prisoner should escape, he longed that it might escape; it tore at his throat and he choked it back in dread and sorrow" (269). Perhaps this incertitude is responsible for his status as less than wholly artist, as if the artist as artist can only exist in a relationship of hostility to the artist as man or woman.

This, then, is the troubled situation at the story's opening, and also at the story's midpoint, for action, here, has taken a definite backseat to description. But action there is, finally, in the classic sense. Even for this Adam there is an Eve, identified here merely as "the Woman," who intrudes one evening at dusk, speaking: "It was the usual story, vulgarly told: admiration for his genius, sympathy with his suffering, only a woman could understand" (270). The isolato's first reaction is fury, but soon he is "struck in spite of himself by the extraordinary pallor of her lips" (270). Other, similar attractions are described, including "a close-fitting hat of faded green felt" (270). The total ensemble rouses the until recently immured semiartist to something like oxymoron: "he thought he had never seen such charming shabbiness" (270).

The woman stays, and returns on subsequent evenings. Her initial departure is attended by ambivalent reflections that are reported in detail: "When at last she went away he felt that something had gone out from him, something he could not spare, but still less could grudge, something of the desire to live" (270). These losses accumulate, each evening with "this woman" costing him "a part of his essential animality" (270), and thus hastening the day when the "implacable caged resentment" (269) within will overwhelm him.

The end, apparently, for the prose here is at once turgid and oblique, a strange mélange, arrives in two stages. The first seems to be sexual: "Until at last, for the first time, he was unconditioned by the Satanic dimensional Trinity, he was released, acheived [*sic*] the blue flower, Vega, GOD." It sounds glorious, but the morning after is a very different matter: "he found himself in his room, spent with ecstasy, torn by the bitter loathing of that which he had condemned to the humanity of silence" (271). This cycle, too, is repeated, so that "each night he died and was God, each night revived and was torn, torn and battered with increasing grievousness" (271).

They could not go on like this, that is clear enough, and stage two of the end arrives in the penultimate paragraph. The woman is looking at "the face that she had overlaid with death" when suddenly "she was swept aside by a great storm of sound," a "triumphant" cry that shook the house, "climbing in a dizzy, bubbling scale, until, dispersed, it fused into the breath of the forest and the throbbing cry of the sea." The final paragraph, after all this rattle and purple, caps the story nicely: "They found her caressing his wild dead hair" (271).

Given some experience with Beckett's later, better known work, it is possible to discern recurrent elements here receiving early exercise. An isolated central character divided against himself and devoted to the "imposition of silence" understood as a specifically artistic feat, a figure "partly artist," partly misogynist, and almost wholly self-absorbed, a deliberately rudimentary "plot" hardly deserving of the word—such features appear again and again in his work. But "Assumption" does not prefigure this later work by any unmistakable sign. It is in every way a young man's story, a young artist's story, a young intellectual's story, brimming with suffering and apotheosis and determinedly transcendent sexuality.

More Pricks than Kicks

Beckett published two stories and one "prose fragment" in 1932. The latter and one of the former are extracts from the unfinished, never published novel *Dream of Fair to Middling Women*, and the other story is an early version of "Dante and the Lobster," which in 1934 would open his first collection of stories, *More Pricks than Kicks*. "Dante and the Lobster" was followed there by nine others, connected each to the other in several ways. All share, for example, their central character, one Belacqua Shuah, who gets his surname from the Bible and his cognomen from Dante's *Purgatorio*, and their physical setting, Dublin and environs. Temporally, they are arranged in sequence, leading from the death of a lobster to the death of the hero, with many deaths in between. Tonally, they are united by a highly self-conscious, allusive style—arch, aggressive, comic.

The stories are mostly comic, in a manner that begins to seem recognizably the author's. "He was telling a funny story about a fiasco" says the narrator of a later story, but the reference to the stories of *More Pricks than Kicks* is precise.[2] They are stories about fiascos—deaths and dismemberments are everywhere in them—and they are very funny. Things begin promptly in "Dante and the Lobster" with the hero, Belacqua, "bogged" in his reading of the opening cantos of the *Paradiso*.[3] Specifically, he cannot follow Beatrice's explanation of moon spots to Dante the pilgrim, and his efforts to do so bear so little fruit that noon, with its call to other duties, comes to him as a relief from this "quodlibet" (a philosophical or theological disputation).

Three obligations organize the remainder of Belacqua's day: "First lunch, then the lobster, then the Italian lesson" (*MPTK*, 10). Lunch, first in line, is presented as a delicate affair, fraught with perils. Many things can go wrong, and if they do, "he might just as well not eat at all, for the food would turn to bitterness on his palate" (*MPTK*, 10). In the first place, he must not be disturbed by any "brisk tattler" bearing either "a big idea or a petition" (*MPTK*, 10); in the second place the bread for his sandwich must be properly toasted, for if there was "one thing he abominated more than another it was to feel his teeth meet in a bathos of pith and dough" (*MPTK*, 11); and in the third place the cheese for the sandwich, to be called for on the way to the "lowly public where he was expected, in the sense that the entry of his grotesque person would provoke no comment or laughter" (*MPTK*, 15), must be not just any cheese but "a good green stenching rotten lump of Gorgonzola cheese" (*MPTK*, 14).

But in the matter of lunch, unlike the matter of Dante's moon spots, Belacqua is successful. He avoids disastrous encounters, with their accompanying "conversational nuisance" (*MPTK*, 13), and the sandwich, cheese, toast, and appropriate spices, no butter, is perfection itself: "his teeth and jaws had been in heaven, splinters of vanquished toast spraying forth at each gnash. It was like eating glass. His mouth burned and ached with the exploit." The lunch, obligation number one, is such a success that "it would abide as a standard in his mind" (*MPTK*, 17). He moves on to obligation number two, the lobster, where other dangers threaten. His "lousy old bitch of an aunt" may not have placed her order in time; the fishmonger may delay him by failing to have the lobster ready. "God damn these tradesmen," Belacqua thinks, "you can never rely on them" (*MPTK*, 16).

But here, again, he is pleasantly surprised—"The lobster was ready after all, the man handed it over instanter"—and he proceeds to obligation number three, the Italian lesson, "quite happy, for all had gone swimmingly" (*MPTK* 17). Of this obligation he has no fears, only eager anticipations. His teacher, Signorina Adriana Ottolenghi, is "so charming and remarkable" that Belacqua has "set her on a pedestal in his mind, apart from other women" (*MPTK*, 16). He is eager to impress her, to "frame a shining phrase" (*MPTK*, 16) in Italian for her, to don "an expression of profundity" in responding to her suggestion that he "might do worse than make up Dante's rare movements of compassion in Hell" (*MPTK*, 19). But these gestures, one begins to notice, are superficial, mere phrases and expressions, far from the heart of the matter, which has to do with "movements of compassion." For in fact

Belacqua responds to the Ottolenghi's suggestion with an incompre-
hension only exacerbated by his "expression of profundity," quoting
what he calls a "superb pun" from the *Inferno*'s twentieth canto: *"qui
vive la pieta quando e ben morta"* (here pity/piety lives when it is thor-
oughly/better dead). This gem, of course, has no relation whatever to
any of "Dante's rare movements of compassion in hell." Belacqua,
busy with his phrases and expressions, preening in the rigged mirror of
his mind, has clearly not heard the Ottolenghi. She has tried to teach
him, even to teach him more than Italian, but without success, as her
response to his citation makes clear:

> She said nothing.
> "Is it not a great phrase?" he gushed.
> She said nothing.
> "Now" he said like a fool "I wonder how you could translate that?"
> Still she said nothing. (*MPTK*, 19)

But Belacqua, poor student, is not the Ottolenghi's only auditor,
fortunately, since her suggestion is preserved in Beckett's story, and,
in fact, broaches that story's major theme. Readers, here as so often in
fiction, drama, and poetry, have the opportunity to be superior to the
hero. In the story's title, Dante shares top billing with a lobster, already
introduced as delivered fresh and on time to the happy Belacqua on
his way from lunch to lesson. In the story's final episode, Belacqua
brings the lobster to his aunt, only to be shocked to learn that it is still
alive and that lobsters are customarily so when cooked. "Have sense,"
says his no-nonsense aunt, "lobsters are always boiled alive. They
must be" (*MPTK*, 22).

The title now makes sense, and the Ottolenghi's lesson deepens.
From Dante's moon spots to the lobster in the pot, from the story's
beginning to the story's end, the message is the same. The moon with
its spots was Cain, "seared with the first stigma of God's pity, that an
outcast might not die quickly" (*MPTK*, 12). The lobster does not die
quickly either. Belacqua, seeing it "exposed cruciform on the oilcloth"
in preparation for the boiling water, consoles himself: "Well, . . . it's
a quick death, God help us all." This easy shuffle, however, equally
available to all eager to distance themselves from the suffering of others, is emphatically rejected in the story's last, stark line: "It is not"
(*MPTK*, 22).

A quick death—its desirability is a hoary theme, found in Sophocles.

Beckett will make its unavailability a cornerstone of his work. In *Waiting for Godot*, for example, Estragon appalls fellow tramp Vladimir by judging his own misfortunes as greater than Christ's. Not only did the latter live in a warm, dry climate, but in that climate "they crucified quick."[4] This advantage is not available in "Dante and the Lobster," not to Cain, not to the lobster, not to the condemned murderer McCabe, the rejection of whose petition for mercy was news that "further spiced" (*MPTK*, 17) Belacqua's lunch, and not to Signorina Adriana Ottolenghi, either, whose final line in the story is a bitter, deep response to Belacqua's casual question, following an interruption:

> "Where were we?" said Belacqua
> But Neapolitan patience has its limits.
> "Where are we ever?" cried the Ottolenghi "where we were, as we were." (*MPTK*, 20)

Where we are, ever, in this story, and in the world Beckett will establish with increasing authority from here on out, is a purgatory verging on hell, a place of more pricks than kicks. This, then, is the basic situation, the given, a world chock-full of suffering and decline, slow decline. When Belacqua returns home to his aunt, she is busy in the garden, "tending whatever flowers die at that time of year" (*MPTK*, 21). She embraces him, and "together they went down into the bowels of the earth, into the kitchen in the basement" (*MPTK*, 21). This is not especially oblique. Even the bread used in preparation of Belacqua's lunch at the beginning of the story is subjected to a slow death. Before toasting, the bread is "spongy and warm, alive." Knowing that toasting "must not on any account be done too rapidly," lest "you only charred the outside and left the pith as sodden as before" (*MPTK*, 11), Belacqua lowers the flame and by his patience produces the desired result, "done to a dead end, black and smoking" (*MPTK*, 12).

In such a world, and to its denizens, various attitudes are possible. The Ottolenghi, against the grain, counsels compassion, and her student, though he misses the lesson, is provoked to introspection by her despairing cry. On his homeward walk, he ponders her words: "Where we were . . . Why not pity and piety both, even down below? Why not mercy and Godliness together? A little mercy in the stress of sacrifice, a little mercy to rejoice against judgment" (*MPTK*, 21). But Belacqua is not ready for such wisdom. Here, as in other stories, he is the receiver of compassion, not the giver, and his aunt is right to scorn his squeamishness. "You make a fuss," she says, "and upset me and then lash into it for your dinner" (*MPTK*, 22). No, the "shining phrase" and the "expression of profundity" are the summits of Belacqua's attainment. The shining action, profundity itself, the true phrase that does not shine—these come (when they come) from others, from the Ottolenghi or the aunt, who appears to provide for Belacqua even as she apparently receives poor gratitude from her nephew, or even from the tradesman (whose "little family grocery" [*MPTK*, 13] supplies Belacqua with his Gorgonzola) who "felt sympathy and pity for this queer customer who always looked ill and dejected" (*MPTK*, 15).

Other stories follow a similar pattern. In "Fingal," the second story, Belacqua concludes a country excursion by abandoning his girlfriend of the moment, Winnie Coates, and fleeing to a pub on a stolen bicycle. The story is memorable for the bicycle, since bicycles fascinate many of Beckett's protagonists, for its introduction of the Portrane Lunatic Asylum as part of the landscape (Belacqua, as he points it out, tells Winnie his heart lives there) since asylums and their inmates reappear even more often than bicycles, and perhaps most of all for one moment between Winnie and Belacqua when she extends to him a compassion that, being unearned, must come as a kind of secular grace.

Learning that a rash on his face is in fact impetigo, Winnie is angered that he has nevertheless kissed her. He offers the excuse of passion, recognizing it as lame:

> "I forgot" he said. "I get so excited you know."
> She spittled on her handkerchief and wiped her mouth. Belacqua lay humbly beside her, expecting her to get up and leave him. But instead she said:
> "What is it anyway? What does it come from?"
> "Dirt" said Belacqua, "you see it on slum children."
> A long awkward silence followed these words.
> "Don't pick it darling" she said unexpectedly at last, "you'll make it worse."
> This came to Belacqua like a drink of water to drink in a dungeon. Her goodwill must have meant something to him. (*MPTK*, 24–25)

It did mean something, perhaps, but not enough to keep him from abandoning Winnie later when the bicycle beckoned.

"Ding-Dong," the collection's third story, features a first-person narrator who identifies himself as Belacqua's former close friend. Following an opening disquisition on Belacqua's devotion to peripeteia—"He was pleased to think that he could give what he called the Furies the slip by merely setting himself in motion" (*MPTK*, 36)—the story is told of an evening made memorable by his purchase, while seated in a pub, of four seats in heaven from "a woman of very remarkable presence" (*MPTK*, 44). This strange event seems consciously to echo *The Tempest*, whence comes also the title, perhaps, from Ariel's song, with Belacqua as the charmed Ferdinand. Certainly the story's close, in which Belacqua "tarried a little to listen to the music" (*MPTK*, 46), encourages the parallel. "Ding-Dong" seems a lighter, even a warmer story than its two predecessors, though here, too, there are crucifixions both fast and slow. Among these are the "trituration" (*MPTK*, 43) of a little girl by a bus and the evening departure of "the blind paralytic who sat all day" (*MPTK*, 39) in his wheelchair, begging alms with the aid of a "placard announcing his distress" (*MPTK*, 40). But the story ends with the woman of "remarkable presence," her countenance "full of light" and bearing "no trace of suffering." From others she had "met with more rebuffs than pence" (*MPTK*, 44), but Belacqua for once responds positively. Perhaps it is significant, too, that his self-centeredness, here called "Ego Maximus, little me" (*MPTK*, 39), is so far moderated that his purchases are on behalf of others—friend, father, mother, mistress—rather than for himself.

"A Wet Night," next in the collection and one of two salvaged more or less directly from *Dream of Fair to Middling Women*, is one of the volume's longest (only "What a Misfortune" is comparable). Its central event is a holiday party, "claret cup and intelligentsia," attended by, among others, Belacqua, late and in sad disrepair, and, arriving earlier, his "current one and only" (*MPTK*, 51), Alba Perdue. The party gathers under one roof a diverse collection of Dublin's poseurs and failures, and all—except the Alba, queen of this and any likely ball—are treated with the narrator's contempt. The hostess, for example, Caleken Frica, first described as a "throttled gazelle," possesses a face "beyond appeal, a flagrant seat of injury," and resembles at last nothing so much as a "martyress in rut" (*MPTK*, 61). Her party, attended by many in the hope of free eats and drinks, and these are disappointed by the meagre spread, soon degenerates into a "sinister kiss-me-Charley hugger-mugger" that "spread like wildfire throughout the building, till it raged from attic to basement" (*MPTK*, 76). Alba, however, holds herself apart from all this.

Meanwhile, Belacqua, moving unsteadily from pub to party in a bitter rain, suddenly feels "white and clammy" (*MPTK*, 70) and leans against a wall. Soon he is accosted by a policeman, only to embarrass himself and anger the lawman by throwing up, "with undemonstrative abundance, all over the boots and trouser-ends of the Guard," who promptly knocks him down "into the outskirts of his own offal" (*MPTK*, 71). Beckett, in passages like this, is finding his voice.

At last Belacqua reaches the party, where "the Alba thought she had never seen anybody, man or woman, look quite such a sovereign booby" (*MPTK*, 78). This is saying something, given the present company, but it does not stop her next movement, any more than his impetigo had earlier stopped Winnie's:

> In an unsubduable movement of misericord the Alba started out of her chair.
> "Nino" she called, without shame or ceremony.
> The distant call came to Belacqua like a pint of Perrier to drink in a dungeon. (*MPTK*, 78)

"A Wet Night," as several critics have pointed out, is on one level an obvious parody of Joyce's famous *Dubliners* story "The Dead," which it echoes in both structure and detail. But the reference—this is important—is not so much a gesture of homage as a comic declaration of independence. The new man, it says, will be doing things differently. Consider the most obvious instance, the echo of Joyce's famous closing description of the "softly falling" snow that is "general all over Ireland," falling "faintly through the universe . . . like the descent of their last end, upon all the living and the dead."[5] "A Wet Night" features rain instead, and it falls not softly but with "a rather desolate uniformity," and not upon the whole universe of the quick and dead but "upon the bay, the littoral, the mountains and the plains, and notably upon the Central Bog" (*MPTK*, 83). What is more, as if the cool, almost meteorological note introduced by "littoral," "uniformity," and "notably" did not sufficiently undercut the lyricism of the original, Beckett makes sure to deprive the passage of the dignity conferred by closure. The last word is given, instead, to Belacqua's early morning departure from the Alba's home, a less than dignified exit in which he throws away his boots—years later, in *Waiting for Godot*, Estragon will also struggle with boots—and is for the second time ordered to move on by a policeman.

"A Wet Night" is notable also for its praise of silence, given as a clinching general question following a relentless savaging, complete with instances of awful conversation, of the Frica's party. "Who shall silence them, at last?" the narrator wants to know; "Who shall circumcise their lips from speaking, at last?" (*MPTK*, 79). Good question, and Beckett has made it his own, has made it of himself, in a tone hovering exactly between assertion and despair.

"Love and Lethe," story number five, is built like "Ding-Dong" on a foolish act that ends in music. Belacqua and yet another lady in his life, this one named Ruby Tough (she is mentioned before her time, in violation of all the norms of sequence and without the slightest apology, in "A Wet Night"), agree to a dual suicide and make careful plans. In this purpose, of course, Belacqua is the instigator, and he "cultivated Ruby" as he cultivates the others, as one cultivates a garden for its calories, "for the part she was to play on his behalf" (*MPTK*, 89). But he is richly supplied with reasons; Belacqua lacks many things but reasons he has aplenty—in this instance "Greek and Roman reasons, Sturm und Drang reasons, reasons metaphysical, aesthetic, erotic, anterotic and chemical, Empedocles of Agrigentum and John of the Cross reasons" (*MPTK*, 90). All of these are false, but Ruby, "flattened by this torrent of incentive" (*MPTK*, 90), agrees anyway, secure in her possession of "an incurable disorder" (*MPTK*, 89) and sensing in Belacqua's silly plan "a chance to end with a fairly beautiful bang" (*MPTK*, 90).

But the plan goes awry, as plans do, especially plans on these pages. The "swagger sports roadster, chartered at untold gold by the hour" (*MPTK*, 90), the aged whiskey purchased "on tick" (*MPTK*, 96), the revolver, ammunition, and poison, all these are squandered to rather more usual ends when "the revolver went off, harmlessly luckily, and the bullet fell *in terram* nobody knows where" (*MPTK*, 99). Instead of dying gloriously under the motto "TEMPORARILY SANE" (*MPTK*, 97) lettered on an old license plate, the would-be self-slaughterers "came together in inevitable nuptial" as the delicate narrator moves "away on tiptoe" (*MPTK*, 99), ending his story in benediction: "May their night be full of music at all events" (*MPTK*, 100). This same narrator recurs more frequently than his predecessors to direct asides, if such things are possible, to the reader. Sometimes these provide helpful information: "Reader, a rosiner is a drop of the hard" (*MPTK*, 86), or, "Reader, a gloria is coffee laced with brandy" (*MPTK*, 87). Sometimes they urge the adequacy of explanations already tendered to the needs of "even the most captious reader" (*MPTK*, 89).

Story number six, "Walking Out," is most memorable for the tramp already extolled, the "real man at last" whose gentle "smile proof against all adversity" (*MPTK*, 104) so abashes the "wretched bourgeois" (*MPTK*, 103) Belacqua. But this is mere interlude in a rush of events "One fateful fine Spring evening" (*MPTK*, 101) that leave that paltry hero beaten and his latest girl Lucy crippled. The beating, a "brutal verberation" (*MPTK*, 113) richly deserved, is administered by an "infuriated Tanzherr" (*MPTK*, 112) on behalf of himself and his "pretty little German girl" (*MPTK*, 109). The walk of the title is at least in part a voyeur's reconnaissance; Belacqua, as Lucy's "horrible diagnosis" (*MPTK*, 109) has only just this same evening made clear, is a "creepy-crawly" (*MPTK*, 108), a "trite spite of the vilest description." The crippling, undeserved, is administered by "a superb silent limousine, a Daimler no doubt, driven by a drunken lord" (*MPTK*, 110), which runs down Lucy, a devoted equestrienne, and her "magnificent jennet" (*MPTK*, 104), as she rides, her mind a court for "cruel battledore" (*MPTK*, 110) between the image of the old Belacqua, loved, and the new, despicable, to the place of their scheduled rendezvous.

Neither arrives, Lucy because of the lord in his Daimler, Belacqua because of the "brutal verberation" of the Tanzherr. But the ending, at least of this story, is all Pippa Passes and Pangloss, since "now he is happily married to Lucy and the question of cicisbei does not arise" (*MPTK*, 113). The question had arisen earlier only at Belacqua's insistence—he had urged her to infidelity on his behalf, even prior to matrimony, just as he had earlier urged Ruby to share his suicide. He knows no other behalf, it seems. These recondite terms, rare even in dictionaries, culled from Latin, Italian, German, "battledore" (Oriental game, source of badminton), "verberation" (lashing with a rod or stick), "cicisbi" (lovers of a married woman or women) and the like—do not worry, reader, they will soon abate.

"What a Misfortune," announcing Lucy's death in its first paragraph, speedily introduces another love (the term is used loosely, as is customary), Thelma bboggs. She is the fifth, after Winnie, Alba, Ruby, and Lucy (the Ottolenghi does not count). Thelma and Belacqua also marry; the preparations for this event occupy the greater part of the story. The parents of the bride, Mr. and Mrs. Otto Olaf bboggs, her sister, Una, "for whom an ape had already been set aside in hell: (*MPTK*, 118), the lover of the bride's mother, Walter Draffin, the groom's best man, Capper Quin, known as Hairy on account of his

13

baldness, the remainder of the groom's entourage, two "deadbeats" (*MPTK*, 128) named Jimmy the Duck Skyrm, "an aged cretin," and Hermione Nautzsche, "a powerfully built nymphomaniac" (*MPTK*, 138)—all these and still more make up the cast of this funniest (and, with "A Wet Night," the longest) story in this funny collection.

And also it's most horrifying—the gentle humor of "Ding-Dong" and "Love and Lethe" are replaced here with something much more harsh. The "misfortune" of the title refers, among other things, to the story's central event, a wedding. To Belacqua, at the moment of falsehood (he is marrying Thelma for her "promissory wad" [*MPTK*, 116]), the church itself is a "cruciform cage, the bulldogs of heaven holding the chancel, the procession about to give tongue in the porch, the transepts cul de sac" (*MPTK*, 138). Except for "Dear Otto Olaf" (*MPTK*, 123), whose gratitude to Walter Draffin for years of service earns him the narrator's respect and sympathy, the story's major characters come in for scathing contempt. Here, for example, is Una, Thelma's older sister: "Think of holy Juliana of Norwich, to her aspect add a dash of souring, to her tissue half a hundredweight of adipose, abstract the charity and prayers, spray in vain with opopanax and assafoetida, and behold a radiant Una" (*MPTK*, 121). Disaster reigns, from large event to small. Thelma dies on her honeymoon, and a nameless car park attendant sustains a broken arm attempting to assist Capper Quin with the borrowed honeymoon car. Alba Perdue, not seen since "A Wet Night," is enlisted as a bridesmaid—an act of deliberate cruelty protested only by Otto Olaf and compounded by her subsequent pairing with Draffin. This is, indeed, a funny, sad story about a fiasco, and this yoking begins to seem increasingly central to Beckett's design. This story, more than the others, begins to resemble the deceptive offering of Prometheus, in Hesiod's *Theogony*, where bare bones are concealed beneath an alluring surface of choice cuts. Under its lavish and exaggerated language, "What a Misfortune," in grotesque characters like Skyrm and Nautzsche, for example, begins to offer that scorched and diminished earth later made famous in *Godot* and *Endgame*. The title, an allusion to Voltaire, is a phrase much loved by the author—he had used it before, in Italian, in a poem, and would use it later, in French, in *Malone Dies*.[6]

The next story, number eight, "The Smeraldina's Billet Doux," is the volume's least impressive and its briefest. It came, like "A Wet Night," from *Dream of Fair to Middling Women*, and before that apparently from a personal letter, the use of which was reportedly resented by the sender's family. (There exists, unfortunately, a biography of Beckett whose author meant the subject no good; she discusses this matter in a shocked, eager tone and in highly speculative detail, asserting, for example, the "verbatim" use of a letter not itself cited.[7] But this sort of thing can only increase one's sympathy for the Tanzherr of "Walking Out." Certainly no one should be encouraged to read the letter—or "The Smeraldina's Billet Doux," for that matter.) It is, as the title suggests, a letter, addressed to Belacqua and written in a mad misspelled sludge of English and German, rich in exclamation, capitalization, and other excesses. The content is simple: the Smeraldina describes her activities and her loneliness, recommends films, and tells Belacqua repeatedly and insistently that she craves his body. Bad news, this, to the Belacqua who considered the crippled Lucy a perfect mate, but prior to her injury considered her so dangerous that he repeatedly urged her to "establish their married life" on what he called the "solid basis" (*MPTK*, 103) of cuckoldry. A similar attitude is one of Otto Olaf's wisdoms, too, in "What a Misfortune." Olaf's horns "sat easily upon him," and he feels nothing but gratitude to Walter Draffin: "Any man who saved him trouble, as Walter had for so many years, could rely on his esteem" (*MPTK*, 120). For a man like Belacqua, the Smeraldina is far too robust, and surely he regarded himself fortunate to have her in Germany, where space could serve the present as injury had served the past.

The two final stories, "Yellow" and "Draff," deal, respectively, with Belacqua's death and burial. The death is by medical misadventure and follows immediately upon the physician's confident self-evaluation, while the burial is by none other than the Smeraldina, now Mrs. Shuah number three, assisted by none other than Capper Quin, the best man of "What a Misfortune," now reduced to successor, after the manner of Walter Draffin.

"Yellow" is devoted mostly to Belacqua's hospital meditations, his search for mental equipoise in a time of stress. He is in for operations on nape and toe, amputations both, and he is frightened: "At twelve sharp he would be sliced open—zeep!—with a bistoury. This was the idea his mind for the moment was in no fit state to entertain" (*MPTK*, 159). In his distress, a paradox from Donne, heaven-sent, reminds him at once of Heraclitus and Democritus, and these in turn provide him with two potential aids. "Was it to be laughter or tears?" (*MPTK*, 163) he asks, and at last he chooses the former, reasoning that the latter would be more open to misinterpretation, ascribed not to a considered

15

philosophical position but "rather to the tumour the size of a brick that he had on the back of his neck" (*MPTK*, 164).

This choice once made, even undermined as it is by second thoughts, "the idea" can be confronted successfully. When Belacqua, like the lobster of the opening story, has only seconds to live, he is at his best: he "swaggered through the antechamber" and "bounced up on the table like a bridegroom" (*MPTK*, 174). An ominous simile, this last, in Mr. Beckett's emerging world. We know by now what happens, and soon, to brides and grooms. It is only part, though a vivid part, of a larger lesson on well-laid plans. Plan to die, says "Love and Lethe," and end up with "inevitable nuptial" (*MPTK*, 99); plan a nuptial and end up dead.

"Draff" concentrates its attention not on Belacqua, who begins the story laid out with a Bible under his chin and ends it laid in a grave "upholstered" with bracken and fern, "all lush, green and most sweet smelling" (*MPTK*, 182), but on his widow, the Smeraldina, who has lost all trace of the German accents so pronounced in "The Smeraldina's Billet Doux." Things end as they began, with references to Dante prominent, though a definite turn for the worse is indicated by their tenor. Where "Dante and the Lobster" opened with Belacqua "stuck in the first of the canti in the moon" (*MPTK*, 9), that is, however stuck, in Paradise, "Draff" has his corpse first measured and dressed by a Mr. Malacoda and later conveyed to its resting ground by a driver named Scarmiglione.

But here, as in Dante, commedia prevails. The Smeraldina soon has Capper Quin in tow, Belacqua himself is laid to rest in the "loveliest little lap of earth you ever saw" (*MPTK*, 182), and the cemetery groundskeeper, who gets the book's last scene, is contented: "He sang a little song, he drank his bottle of stout, he dashed away a tear, he made himself comfortable" (*MPTK*, 191). Even Belacqua's house, which is set ablaze by the gardener during his funeral, turns out to be insured. An obnoxious Parson is abandoned on the road after the burial, evicted from the car by Quin, and the servant Mary Ann is raped by the pyromaniac gardener, but these are small matters, that are given short shrift in the story's economy. "Little remains to be told," says the narrator, moving to wrap things up: "On their return they found the house in flames, the home to which Belacqua had brought three brides a raging furnace. It transpired that during their absence something had snapped in the brain of the gardener, who had ravished the servant girl and then set the premises on fire" (*MPTK*, 189).

It is, of course, a part of the story's harsh comedy to undercut such melodrama by so offhanded an introduction, presenting it as the draff of "Draff." ("Draff" is dregs, slop for hogs, lees, what is left of malt after brewing, garbage.) The reader, shocked by a narrator not so much unreliable, though he is that, as unfeeling, may think back to other matters judged too "little" to be told at all. What happens, for example, to the aunt who provided shelter and dinner in "Dante and the Lobster"? Or to the Ottolenghi? Or to Alba Perdue, perhaps aptly named, who after disappearing with Walter Draffin in "What a Misfortune," is mentioned briefly as dead "in the natural course of being seen home" (*MPTK*, 175) at the beginning of "Draff"? This closing story is also notable for the volume's most savage image, a description of the Smeraldina and Quin embracing in shared grief, meeting for the first time after Belacqua's death. They embrace to console, widow and ex–best man, but also in self interest, Wife of Bath to Jenkin, and the narrator seems to view this development with extreme distaste: "Capper Quin arrived on tiptire, in a car of his very own. He grappled with the widow, he simply could not help it. She was a sensible girl in some ways, she was not ashamed to let herself go in the arms of a man of her own weight at last. They broke away, carrot plucked from tin of grease" (*MPTK*, 179–80). Amidst his many bows to Dante, Beckett includes more than one nod to Swift's darker muse.

More Pricks than Kicks, oscillating between such varying shades, from a gentle humor praised in one review as "the profound *risolino* that does not destroy"[8] to the harsher genres characterized in *Watt* as "modes of ululation,"[9] offers two basic challenges to readers. The first is superficial, having to do with the volume's recondite, multilingual vocabulary, the youthful author wearing his learning like a sash of medals, and requires only a bank of dictionaries for its solution. (A branch of this challenge, even less important than the main trunk, has to do with the thick, if not rich, allusiveness of the young man's exuberant prose. If you have read "The Dead," recognize the Beresina as a Byelorussian river and Dr. Petrie as Flinders, archaeologist and Egyptologist, and/or can boast familiarity with the landmarks of Dublin and environs—you may applaud yourself. If you have not, do not worry. Little is lost, in your reading of these stories, and their teller, finding his own voice, his own world, will soon lighten the allusive and referential load.)

The second challenge, anyway, is more worth one's time, as it gets to the heart of not only these but later, better stories. It has to do with

17

tone, with that tightrope along pain and pleasure, tragedy and comedy, pricks and kicks, which is even here Beckett's special métier. Already present, for instance, at the extreme of distance and frigid authority, is that impersonal voice out of the heavens, speaking in fiat and inquisition, that in the beginning rejects Belacqua's sorry bromide on the lobster's death and in the end gives similar brief shrift to his anticipated posthumous encounter with "the girls, Lucy especially, hallowed and transfigured beyond the veil. What a hope!" sneers the voice, "Death had already cured him of that naivete" (*MPTK*, 181). Subsequent works will further embody this imperious otherness—it acquires female gender in *Eh Joe* and even shifts from speaking to listening in *Not I*.

Slightly more personal but no less authoritative is the voice occasionally heard in direct address to the reader in mockery of storytelling's conventions, as, for example, in the instances already cited from "Love and Lethe," or this, from "Dante and the Lobster": "Let us call it Winter, that dusk may fall now and a moon rise" (*MPTK*, 20). This is also the voice of the mock-helpful, mock-learned footnotes, five in number. Finally, as noted and emphasized here by way of compensation for usual neglect, there is the very occasional voice of open and undisguised affirmation, as in the sketch of the tinker in "Walking Out."

Hearing these voices, learning to discount them, when and by how much, learning, too, to notice the omitted voice, the discarded character, the unstated conclusion and unspoken judgment—these are the skills to cultivate when exploring Beckett's stories. For the considerable armamentarium deployed so ostentatiously and aggressively in *More Pricks than Kicks* is radically curtailed in its successors. Before those successors, however, with their very different delights, there is one last early story to consider.

"A Case in a Thousand"

"A Case in a Thousand" appeared in the August 1934 issue of *The Bookman* and has never been reprinted. Like the earlier "Assumption," it moves through a a series of mostly unhappy events to an obliquely triumphant conclusion. A young doctor named Nye, identified at the beginning as "one of the sad men," is summoned for consultation by a surgeon colleague named Bor. The patient, after Bor had "operated with the utmost success," had exhibited "an unfathomable tendency to sink."[10] But here is the complication, a coincidence: the patient, a boy named Bray, is the son of Nye's "old nurse," a woman "whom as a baby and small boy he had adored" (242). And in this old relationship there was a moment that still lives, the memory of which stirs "shame" in Mrs. Bray and makes Dr. Nye's initial recognition something to be "feared" (242). A later story, "The Expelled," refers in passing to a similar situation: "He gave me a woman's name that I've forgotten. Perhaps she had dandled me on her knees while I was still in swaddling clothes and there had been some lovey-dovey. Sometimes that suffices" (*STN*, 19). But this very likely has little bearing, if any, on Mrs. Bray and Dr. Nye.

The events of the present are no better. Bor will operate again only at Nye's urging, and "from the strictly pathological point of view there was as much to be urged on the one side as there was on the other" (242). Nye, therefore, is "outside the scope of his science" but obliged nonetheless to reach a decision. His procedure in this difficult situation is described at some length: "He took hold of the boy's wrist, stretched himself all along the edge of the bed and entered the kind of therapeutic trance that he reserved for such happily rare dilemmas" (242). His expression at this time, "at once aghast and rapt," is witnessed by Mrs. Bray and triggers her recollection of their previous intimacy. The "trance" results in a decision to operate again, but young Bray's lung collapses and he dies. The mother, who has watched at her son's bedside (and outside the hospital in the intervals between visiting hours) throughout his illness, offers Dr. Nye her thanks, but despite "great efforts to speak their minds," they can share only "silence." Nye then leaves for "a short holiday at the seaside" (242).

He is soon called back, however, by a note from Bor, who tells him Mrs. Bray is back at her stand, maintaining the same vigil she had earlier mounted on behalf of her son. He goes to see her and at last broaches the subject that matters: "There's something I've been wanting to ask you." She answers, "I wonder would that be the same thing I've been wanting to tell you ever since that time you stretched out on his bed." (242). It is, of course, and when he replies only by asking if she can "go on," that bedrock question, she relates "a matter connected with his earliest years, so trivial and intimate that it need not be enlarged on here, but from the elucidation of which Dr. Nye, that sad man, expected great things" (242). Unlike Nye, we do not learn what the matter is, but we do know what we need to know: that Mrs. Bray and Dr. Nye, by their persistence and courage, quite outside the scope of his science or any science, have earned their communion. The patient dies, and the doctor is cured. "Thank you very much" he says when Mrs. Bray finishes, "that was what I was wondering" (242). It is a case in a thousand, take that either way—that it is just one case of a thousand equally compelling, emphasizing its universality, or that it is a rare and unique occurrence, emphasizing its rarity, like what happened to Hamlet or Oedipus. Or take it both ways, as intended, no doubt.

Critics have mostly ignored this story, and such comment as it has elicited has focused on its possible sources in Beckett's relationship with his analyst and/or his mother.[11] This is lamentable, since "A Case in a Thousand" presents its muted personae, Dr. Nye and Mrs. Bray, in a style at great remove from the "white voice" (*MPTK*, 148) and "shining phrase" (*MPTK*, 16) of Belacqua. Silence, as a voice in Beckett's writing, is ascending its footstool. In his sympathy with such creatures, with their tendency to stasis and vigil, their stammering difficulty in the attempt to "speak their minds" (242), he is finding a way to speak his own mind, or perhaps merely to speak.

In the big world, however, as the 1930s end and the fledgling author gets his first novel published (*Murphy*, in 1938), a war is coming on. Beckett's life will be spared, but it will be a near miss. Close friends will perish. He will find it necessary to flee his home. All this will affect his work much as the soft bread in "Dante and the Lobster" is changed at Belacqua's hand: "But he would very soon take that plush feel off it, by God but he would very quickly take that fat white look off its face" (*MPTK*, 11). Beckett's next short fictions, four stories written in 1945 and 1946, are harrowed and muted far beyond anything envisioned in *More Pricks than Kicks* and give a "fat white look," indeed, to their prewar predecessors. "A Case in a Thousand" is a step, a modest step, in that direction.

Stories and Texts

Stories

Despite its title, "The End" is very much a beginning. The first of four stories written in 1946, it was published that year (incompletely, owing to editorial misunderstanding, and under the title "Suite") in the July issue of *Temps Modernes*. It was written in French, a new beginning of the most obvious sort, and it was Beckett's first published fiction in the language he was also using at this time in the novel *Mercier and Camier,* and the language he would soon employ in the works that would eventually bring him considerable fortune and even more fame. "The End" was also a monologue, unlike the novel but like "The Expelled" and "The Calmative," two other stories from 1946 that were printed along with it as the *Stories* of *Stories and Texts for Nothing* in 1967, and like "First Love," also from 1946 but not published in English until 1974.

The story opens in utter simplicity, with nothing of "canti in the moon" or the like. "They clothed me and gave me money," says the first-person narrator, taking himself twice as object. "I knew what the money was for, it was to get me started," he continues, confident in his knowing. But he is a realist, too, and a recognizer of limits, even his own: "When it was gone I would have to get more, if I wanted to go on" (*STN*, 47). How nice to have a pragmatist, a regular man of the world, for a narrator, after the hapless Belacqua. And how nice to have characters, too, with real names, some of them, Mr. Weir and Mrs. Maxwell, instead of grotesques with names like Otto Olaf bboggs.

Such comforts continue. It turns out soon enough that the collective "they" operate a "charitable institution" from which the narrator, after an extended stay, is being evicted. He is reluctant to go, in fact he begs to remain, even suggesting a willingness to "make myself useful." But Mr. Weir is not to be dissuaded: "Never come back here whatever you do, you would not be let in. Don't go to any of our branches either, they would turn you away" (*STN*, 49). Other maneuvers by the indigent meet with like responses. He asks for the return of his hat and greatcoat, only to learn that "they had burnt them, together with my other clothes" (*STN*, 47). He claims great age, only to be told that he is "not so old as all that" (*STN*, 56). By such signs as these, even before the story is properly under way, the narrator understands "that the end was near, at least fairly near" (*STN*, 47). Hamm will open *Endgame* with a similar statement, with similar qualification, and with similar inaccuracy.

For what begins to dawn, very soon, on the reader and the narrator is an awareness of a fundamental uncertainty beneath the confident syntactic surface. The narrator seeks a reprieve on account of great age. The claim is rejected, but nothing is learned about his age. Mr. Weir gives the evictee permission to "wait in the cloister till six o'clock," assuring him at the same time that "the rain will go on all day" (*STN*, 50). The rain stops in the following paragraph, and the narrator is evicted from the cloister. The time is not given. Outside, after witnessing a shocking exchange between a small boy and his mother (How can the sky be blue? the boy asks. "Fuck off" (*STN*, 50), she replies), the now homeless indigent first observes that the city "seemed greatly changed," but almost immediately he adds that the "general impression was the same as before" (*STN*, 51). Remembering just after his departure that he has forgotten to ask for a piece of bread, he decides not to return because "I never turned back on such occasions" (*STN*, 51). This seems to be a fundamental principle, repeated not only here but in "The Expelled" as well, but it is nonetheless abrogated soon enough. "I must have read somewhere, when I was small and still read, that it is better not to look back when leaving. And yet I sometimes did" (*STN*, 53–54).

But these uncertainties and inconsistencies seem not to trouble the narrator unduly, indeed, he sometimes acknowledges them with considerable panache. In the days following his eviction, for example, during his search for lodging, he is pleased to report the perfection of "a method of doffing my hat at once courteous and discreet, neither servile nor insolent" (*STN*, 52). He cannot simply sweep his hat off like a swaggering gallant, not "with my skull in the state it was" (*STN*, 48). Instead he "slipped it smartly forward, held it a second poised in such a way that the person addressed could not see my skull, then slipped it back" (*STN*, 52). A definitive solution, it seems, presented as a matter for self-congratulation: "To do that naturally, without creating an unfavorable impression, is no easy matter" (*STN*, 52). But very soon, and without explanation, another solution is posited, only to be speedily withdrawn, and the issue left unresolved. "I subsequently solved this problem," he says, "always fundamental in times of adversity, by wearing a kepi and saluting in military fashion, no, that must be wrong, I don't know, I had my hat at the end" (*STN*, 53). (That the word "kepi," though Beckett's narrators of 1946 like it and use it again in "First Love," stands out as recondite in "The End" is another measure of the story's distance from those of the 1930s, where it would have gone unnoticed in the macaronic blizzard.)

The action of "The End," such as it is, without end at all, may be described in eight stages, alternating without strict regularity between periods of stasis and movement, the former being much preferred to the latter, and between periods of urban and suburban versus rural residence, no great preference being given to either. First there is the eviction from the charitable institution, a place the narrator eulogizes with great feeling: "I saw the familiar objects," he reports, "companions of so many bearable hours. The stool, for example, dearest of all. The long afternoons together, waiting for it to be time for bed" (*STN*, 49). Next comes a period of wandering, searching for new shelter. The first night is spent on a public bench near a watering trough for horses provided (the trough, not the bench) by the philanthropy of Mrs. Maxwell. The bench is sufficiently familiar to be described possessively— "My bench was still there" (*STN*, 51)—but after the "bearable hours" in the institution its comforts seem cold: "I longed to be under cover again, in an empty place, close and warm, with artificial light, an oil lamp for choice, with a pink shade for preference. From time to time someone would come to make sure I was all right and needed nothing. It was long since I had longed for anything and the effect on me was horrible" (*STN*, 52). (This is old wisdom, in Beckett's work, though its statement here, in keeping with the general cooling of rhetorical air, is less portentous. Murphy, on the other hand, citing with only slight error of omission an obscure Cartesian, raises the longing to abstain from longing to the status of principle: "In the beautiful Belgo-Latin of Arnold Geulincx: *Ubi nihil vales, ibi nihil velis*."[12] Geulincx is mentioned briefly in "The End," as well, his *Ethics* having been presented to the narrator by his tutor.)

A third stage finds the unnamed narrator/protagonist once again sheltered, in a basement room rented by a woman of self-described tolerance and benevolence. "My oddities, that's the expression she used,

23

did not alarm her," he says, adding that she told him "with a great deal of feeling, that she would never put me out in bad weather" (*STN*, 53). Narrative uncertainties persist—the nationality of the landlady is "Greek, I think, or Turkish" (*STN*, 53), and the voice that sings "every evening at the same hour, somewhere above me" is first presented as surely young though of unknown gender, a "little girl, unless it was a little boy" (*STN*, 55). Even this certitude soon vanishes, however, in other possibilities: "Was it a song in my head or did it merely come from without?" (*STN*, 55) Merely? A succinct indication, this, of the relative value of what Murphy called the little world, the world of the mind, and the "blooming buzzing confusion" (*M*, 4) of the macrocosm.

But things are better for our narrator in the basement: "I was comfortable enough in this house, I must say" (*STN*, 54). Unfortunately, he is soon evicted again and finds himself in worse straits than ever. Whereas the "charitable institution" gave him money, the landlady cheats him by offering, even as she sells the house and prepares to leave, a reduced rate in exchange for payment six months in advance. The buyer, understandably, "requested me to get up and leave his house immediately. He was most correct, I must say" (*STN*, 56). Specific reasons for the new owner's haste are provided: "He said he needed the room immediately for his pig which even as he spoke was catching cold in a cart before the door" (*STN*, 56). This is an indication, succinct again, of the relative value of man and pig. Remember Mrs. Maxwell and the chosen beneficiaries of her largesse.

Another period of wandering, some of it in rural settings, follows this second eviction: "I don't know how long I wandered thus, resting now in one place, now in another, in the city and in the country" (*STN*, 58). One day he sees his son, maybe—"I was almost certain it was he" (*STN*, 58). No meeting occurs, however, except for a formal bow from the son, which does not impress the father: "He went bustling along on his duck feet, bowing and scraping and flourishing his hat left and right. The insufferable son of a bitch" (*STN*, 58). The attachments of family life, here and elsewhere, in "First Love," for example, are fraught with tension. "Fuck off," says mother to son; "son of a bitch," says father to son. Only the connection of son to father, in these stories, is a generally positive one, was once a generally positive one.

A third shelter is found when " a man I had known in former times" offers to share the "cave by the sea" where he lives with an ass for companion and coworker, the pair making their modest living selling "sand, sea-wrack, and shells to the townsfolk, for their gardens" (*STN*, 58). This period, again, is an interval of respite, beginning from the moment they escape the town on assback, jeered and stoned by little boys and accused by a policeman of disturbing the peace: "We followed the quiet, dustwhite inland roads with their hedges of hawthorn and fuchsia and their footpaths fringed with wild grass and daisies" (*STN*, 59). The cave itself "was nicely arranged, I must say" (*STN*, 59), and his host is a "kind" man who provides exactly the care his guest had longed for on the bench by the horse trough. The repeated phrasing—"to make sure I was all right and needed nothing"—emphasizes the point.

The departure from this haven, too, is different in that it is compelled by no external authority. "I couldn't bear the sea," the sensitive guest complains, and eventually he inquires of his host concerning possible alternatives: "You wouldn't know of a lake dwelling?" (*STN*, 60). What is this host, anyway, a real estate agent? No, the host has nothing in lake dwellings, only other caves and a "cabin in the mountains," which he offers. There is no understanding these tastes, he muses: "And to think I couldn't live anywhere else, he said, in my cabin in the mountains I was very unhappy" (*STN*, 60). This dwelling, it turns out, is quite derelict, its door gone, the glass from the window also, the roof fallen in and the floor "strewn with excrements, both human and animal, with condoms and vomit. In a cowpad a heart had been traced, pierced by an arrow" (*STN*, 61). Here, on "a bed of ferns, gathered at great labour with my own hands," the indigent shelters, free at least from the sea, and saved in a crisis—"One day I couldn't get up"—by a cow. "I tried to suck her," he says, "without much success. Her udder was covered with dung" (*STN*, 61).

Dragged from the shelter by the cow, his opportunities for gradual domestication and utilization of it and other cows lost by his rash approach, the indigent finds himself on a road "all downhill," headed back into town: "Soon there were carts, but they all refused to take me up. In other clothes, with another face, they might have taken me up. I must have changed, since my expulsion from the basement" (*STN*, 62). He has changed, and for the worse. His face, especially, has deteriorated: "A mask of dirty old hairy leather, with two holes and a slit" (*STN*, 62). But this is mere surface. In the world Beckett is building, every collapse, every decline, is at least a blessing in its deadening of one's vulnerability to external assaults and at most an omen of the end, a blessed assurance of eventual extinction. Moran, in *Molloy*, and Dan Rooney in *All That Fall*, are eloquent on this point. "To be literally incapable of motion at last," says Moran, "that must be something! My mind swoons when I think of it. And mute into the bargain! And perhaps deaf as a post! And who knows blind as a bat! And as likely as not your memory a blank! And just enough brain intact to allow you to exult!"[13]

Here, in the story's penultimate section, the newly blessed devotes himself with considerable ingenuity and some success to begging. Detailed descriptions of the tools of this trade, improvised in accord with equally detailed psychological considerations, are provided without the self-conscious denigration usual with other topics. The same narrator who often abandons descriptions in disgust ("Only the ground-floor windows—no, I can't" [*STN*, 67] or dismisses them once finished ("That's all a pack of lies I feel" [*STN*, 51], or "I should never have mentioned them" [*STN*, 63]), here lavishes proud attention on the "board or tray" (*STN*, 64) he devises for begging and pronounces at length on the proper methods for a successful career in this field: "I leaned against the wall, but without nonchalance, I shifted my weight from one foot to the other and my hands clutched the lapels of my coat. To beg with your hands in your pockets makes a bad impression, it irritates the workers, especially in winter. You should never wear gloves either" (*STN*, 65). There is considerable satiric bite, in all this, as in the no less detailed meditation on the proxemics of charity, where too close is a problem ("he was in danger of touching"), and too far is another problem ("But people who give alms don't much care to toss them, there's something contemptuous about this gesture which is repugnant to sensitive natures" (*STN*, 64), leaving only a narrow range for the perfect beggar/giver interaction: "What they like above all is to sight the wretch from afar, get ready their penny, drop it in their stride and hear the God bless you dying away in the distance" (*STN*, 64). But narrative ease and pride, not satiric bite, is the point here. In begging, it seems clear, this misfit who was unable to make himself useful to Mr. Weir has at last found something of a true calling. "Once at my post I did not leave it till nightfall" (*STN*, 65), he says, like any proud professional. He speaks of the alms he receives as "earned," and he understands the time spent in their receipt as "work." He is a success, too: "I even managed to put a little aside, for my very last days." He has even found shelter again, in a riverside shed on "a private estate, or what had once been a private estate" (*STN*, 67). Inside the shed is a boat, which he encloses, making it into a strikingly coffinlike bed. The resulting situation is described in the by now familiar syntax of contentment: "I was very snug in my box, I must say" (*STN*, 69–70).

But the "very last days" do not arrive, not in "The End." (They do not arrive in *Endgame*, either.) The story ends, instead, in "visions," in the narration of interior rather than exterior events. The final paragraph, in a warm-up for *The Unnamable*, runs five pages. "I knew they were visions," he reports, "because it was night and I was alone in my boat" (*STN*, 71). The "vision" itself has two centers, both set in the boat as it floats downriver into "the choppy waters of the bay." One is retrospective, nostalgic, centered on the memory of his father: "I saw the beacons, four in all, including a lightship. I knew them well, even as a child I had known them well. It was evening, I was with my father on a height, he held my hand. I would have liked for him to draw me close with a gesture of protective love, but his mind was on other things. He also taught me the names of the mountains" (*STN*, 71).

The other center, in the visionary present, details a carefully planned suicide: "I must have pierced a hole beforehand in the floorboards, for there I was down on my knees prying out the plug with my knife" (*STN*, 72). Also provided for this occasion are a chain, previously unmentioned, and "my calmative" (*STN*, 72), apparently the contents of "the phial" (*STN*, 59) found during the sojourn in the cave, before that apparently missed by Mr. Weir in the general confiscation, and before that apparently presented to the narrator/hero of "The Calmative" in exchange for a kiss. The chain has been fastened around the suicide's waist and attached to the boat's bow, the calmative will be swallowed, and, in a spectacular contraction/explosion reminiscent of the apotheosis of "Assumption," the "sea, the sky, the mountains and the islands closed in and crushed me in a mighty systole, then scattered to the uttermost confines of space" (*STN*, 72). The "vision" within the story at this point opens on the "memory" of another story, "the story I might have told, a story in the likeness of my life, I mean without the courage to end or the strength to go on" (*STN*, 72). Story into vision into memory—"The End," having opened in closure, here closes in shifting perspectives and the introduction of alternatives. The last word, as in *The Unnamable*, is "on."

"The Expelled," like "The End," opens with the narrator's ejection, this time from a three-story house with "a massive green door," and includes an account of his subsequent search for shelter. Like his predecessor, he loves flowers, oil lamps, and stables, is stopped twice by policemen, entertains memories of his father, is given money in return for his signature, claims never to look back when leaving but sometimes does, and closes with the consideration of alternative stories. It is tempting to take both narrators for one hero, so similar are the two vagabonds, although if there is just one hero, he apparently appears at an earlier date in "The Expelled," since he still has his greatcoat. This later story is briefer, too, and limits itself to the transcription of one day's misadventures, one cycle of stasis and movement, shelter and homelessness. Here, instead of a hospitable cavedweller and his ass, a cabman and his horse provide shelter, especially the horse, since the guest elects to sleep in the stable.

Once again, the sheltered times and places are praised. "How beautiful it was!" he exclaims of the house, "There were geraniums in the windows. I have brooded over geraniums for years" (*STN*, 12). The story's most lyric passage is devoted to the lighting, by the cabman and his passenger, of the cab's oil lamps: "I asked him if I might light the second lamp, since he had already lit the first himself. He gave me his box of matches, I swung open on its hinges the little convex glass, lit and closed at once, so that the wick might burn steady and bright snug in its little house, sheltered from the wind. I had this joy" (*STN*, 22). Lucky man, and lucky wick, safe and warm in "its little house." (*Watt*, written earlier, includes in its "Addenda" the image of a less lucky light, "a flame with dark winds hedged about" [*W*, 250].) In striking contrast to this loving attention to geraniums and oil lamps is this same narrator's hostility to more standard recipients, at least in legend, of love and attention. Forced to "fling myself to the ground to avoid crushing a child," for example, he is careful to dissociate himself from any commendable intent: "I would have crushed him gladly, I loathe children, and it would have been doing him a service, but I was afraid of reprisals" (*STN*, 15). This same fall, however, knocks down "an old lady covered with spangles and lace, who must have weighed about sixteen stone." (A stone is a unit of weight, most often but not always understood as equalling fourteen pounds.) "I had high hopes she had broken her femur," he notes, adding that "old ladies break their femur easily, but not enough, not enough" (*STN*, 15).

"The Expelled," in light of preoccupations evident in other stories, is noteworthy on several additional counts. One is the description of the narrator's bizarre walk; another is his momentary temptation to pyromania. The walk, marked by "Stiffness of the lower limbs, as if nature had denied me knees, extraordinary splaying of the feet to right and left of the line of march" (*STN*, 13), is in essence the walk described at much greater length in *Watt* and summarized there as a "funambulistic stagger" (*W*, 31). The temptation to pyromania is also recurrent, indulged by the gardener in "Draff," for example, and also by Mr. Madden in *Mercier and Camier*. Finally, there are the same repeated deprecations of narrative's requirements, or of their particular fulfillment, and a sufficiently persistent use of biblical and Christian allusion to alert readers with an interest in that sort of thing. "So much for that description" (*STN*, 12), he says, as if giving up in disgust, but then the description (in this instance of a door) continues for several lines. In another instance (this one concerning his hat), the comment comes first: "How describe this hat? And why?" And he does not. "Some other time," he says, "some other time" (*STN*, 11).

The Christian echoes are mostly unobtrusive, even plausibly inadvertent, but not with this writer, as for example in the narrator's reference in "The Expelled" to the time "when I was still in swaddling clothes" (*STN*, 19), or in "The End" the reference to an orator's addressing the hero as a "crucified bastard" (*STN*, 67), or his description of stables as "my salvation" (*STN*, 57). But sometimes the allusion is more extended. For example: "I raised my eyes to the sky, whence cometh our help" (*STN*, 13). That is "The Expelled," but it is used again (twice) in "The Calmative." Both strategies, the brief reference and the more extended citation, are employed by Beckett on other occasions. Hamm's "It's finished,"[14] for example, at the beginning of *Endgame*, would be obvious to most, but the title of *All That Fall* might be unobtrusive to many until its meaning becomes obvious in the text.

In "First Love," once again, the same derelict narrator seems to be at work, manipulating the same props. Flowers, an oil lamp, a greatcoat, a tutor, memories of father, songs barely heard, a bench, an abandoned shed or cabin where declarations of love may be found inscribed on "old cowshit"[15]—all these are present, and many others. This is the same story of eviction and search for shelter, of departure from shelter offered. Perhaps the basic story, after all, of expulsion from womb and subsequent agitated search for tomb, told again by a reluctant teller with occasional pauses to despise his efforts. "I'm sick and tired of this name Lulu," he says, "I'll give her another, more like her, Anna for example" (*FL*, 22). A betterment, perhaps, a step toward closer similitude? No. The very possibility, and the possibility of its significance, is rejected immediately: "it's not more like her but no matter" (*FL*,

22). Elsewhere, such negative judgments are more general: "I see no connexion between these remarks" (*FL*, 21).

In "First Love," too, more obviously than in the other stories, eviction and expulsion are presented in a figurative light. "What goes by the name of love," for instance, "is banishment, with now and then a postcard from the homeland" (*FL*, 18). When one loves, that is, especially if one's love is "the priapic one" (*FL*, 22), perhaps, one is subject to the most basic eviction: "One is no longer oneself, on such occasions, and it is painful to be no longer oneself, even more painful if possible than when one is" (*FL*, 18). Fortunately, given this assessment, the condition is curable. One need only associate with the beloved; proximity will guarantee contempt. The action of "First Love" may be understood as illustrating this protocol. The narrator, evicted and given money following his father's death, is stretched upon a bench when he is approached by a woman, Lulu, a prostitute. "Shove up" (*FL*, 17), she says, by way of greeting, and soon escalates to singing folk songs and "stroking my ankles" (*FL*, 18).

Verbal dissuasions proving futile, the victim of these attentions flees, seeking "refuge in a deserted cowshed." But mere distance is not enough: "It was in this byre . . . that for the first time in my life . . . I had to contend with a feeling which gradually assumed, to my dismay, the dread name of love" (*FL*, 21). That this is the correct name is never certain, since love is a new experience to this derelict—no wonder his family threw him out!—but he knows of it secondhand, having "heard of the thing, at home, in school, in brothel and church, and read romances, in prose and verse, under the guidance of my tutor, in six or seven languages, both dead and living, in which it was handled at length" (*FL*, 22). Various kinds of love—not only the priapic, but also the platonic and the intellectual—are suggested and rejected as applying to the present instance. But taxonomy, to one in such a state of disturbance, is of secondary importance. Therapeutics is what matters: "In order to put an end, to try and put an end, to this plight, I returned one evening to the bench" (*FL*, 23).

Lulu is still about—"I told you she was a highly tenacious woman" (*FL*, 24)—and soon takes him to her rooms, complete with oil lamp, where he prepares a shelter by emptying one room of its furniture, leaving only a sofa, which he faces toward the back wall and climbs in, "like a dog into its basket." They discuss the location of the "convenience" (*FL*, 30), the lack of a chamberpot, the presence of running water and gas, and the absence of electricity. All this proximity and "conversation worthy of the name" (*FL*, 27) has the desired effect: "Already my love was waning, that was all that mattered. Yes, already I felt better, soon I'd be up to the slow descents again, the long submersions, so long denied me through her fault" (*FL*, 30–31). This sounds like he wants a bath and resents Lulu's protracted occupancy of the facilities, but the nature of these yearnings has already been specified. "I did not feel easy when I was with her," he admits, "but at least free to think of something else than her, of the old trusty things, and so little by little, as down steps toward a deep, of nothing" (*FL*, 27–28). What he is after, this narrator, is not scuba diving or spelunking but what the Unnamable, in the near future, will call "the bliss of coma" (*TN*, 325).

A generally satisfactory routine is soon established, bringing another period of stasis, with its usual perquisites and only minor disadvantages. "She brought my meals at the appointed hours," he says, clear echoes of "The End" sounding here, "looked in now and then to see if all was well and make sure I needed nothing" (*FL*, 31). The minor disadvantages include an occasional "night of love" (*FL*, 31) (or perhaps there is only one) and, also occasional, the "sound of singing." It is too good to last, this setup, and it does not last. First, there is the "groan and giggle" (*FL*, 32) of Lulu's customers, unavoidable for two reasons, she tells him in response to a complaint: "We live by prostitution," and "They can't help but yap and yelp." He says he will "have to leave" (*FL*, 33), but he does not.

Then, as if "yap and yelp" are not bother enough, Lulu adds cries uttered during childbirth, at the end of a pregnancy whose origin she attributes to her lover. Guest? Charge? At any rate it is too much. "What finished me was the birth," he says. Not a word or a worry for Lulu; though he does give some thought to what "that infant must have been going through" (*FL*, 35). The putative father leaves, despite the oncoming winter, despite the needs of the child and the mother, at the time at least temporarily unable to "live by prostitution." Their needs do not cross his mind. "I hesitated to leave, the leaves were falling already, I dreaded the winter" (*FL*, 34), he says, adding that "It went to my heart to leave a house without being put out" (*FL*, 35). Later, in another passage of undefended lyricism, he admits he was wrong to worry about the winter: "One should not dread the winter, it too has its bounties, the snow gives warmth and deadens the tumult and its pale days are soon over. But I did not yet know, at that time, how tender the earth can be for those who have only her and how many graves in her giving, for the living" (*FL*, 34–35).

So ends first love, in renewed flight, from the rooms as earlier from the bench. The flight, this time, is from cries, a baby's cries, a mother's cries. But mere time, added to mere distance, is not enough. "For years I thought they would cease," the lover admits. "Now I don't think so any more" (*FL*, 36). Perhaps love is incurable, after all. The action of "First Love," and specifically the close, which once again considers alternatives, may be understood as illustrating this point: "I could have done with other loves perhaps. But there it is, either you love or you don't" (*FL*, 36).

"The Calmative" is different. The several obvious similarities—the narrator is a grotesque who wears a greatcoat, remembers his father, and despises his own storytelling—are finally less striking than its structural and stylistic outrages, which are handled with great panache. More persistently than in the other stories, the narrative line in "The Calmative" is sabotaged. The solidities of setting are dissolved without warning, characters appear and disappear in crowds. For example: emerging from the "little wood" (*STN*, 29) that apparently holds his "refuge" (*STN*, 28), and "having crossed the ditch that girdles it" on his apparently solitary way through a pasture, the narrator suddenly interrupts this itinerary to present a remarkably incongruous scene: "What I saw was a bald man in a brown suit, a comedian" (*STN*, 29). In what was just moments ago, lines ago, a pasture, he envisions not only a comedian, but also an audience to appreciate his ribaldries: "The women seemed even more entertained than their escorts, if that were possible. Their shrill laughter pierced the clapping. . . . Perhaps they had in mind the reigning penis sitting who knows by their side" (*STN*, 29). But then, just as the reader adjusts, makes a stage, perhaps a whole cabaret, in the midst of a pasture, the comedian and his audience disappear, not to return. So much for nature's mirror, for what Beckett referred to in *Proust* as "the vulgarity of a plausible concatenation."[16] Soon enough, after another, less abrupt digression concerning the bedtime stories of the narrator's father, about "Joe Breem, or Breen, the son of a lighthouse-keeper" (*STN*, 30), the remembered pasture is restored, and with it the conventions of calming stories. But one victim, one target of Beckett's humor, would seem to be such conventions, the laughably inadequate tools of his storyteller's trade, sufficient at best for lulling a child to sleep. But is this such an unworthy end?—this counterquestion would also seem to be present, suggested by the meditation on the Joe Breem stories. Those stories ended, after all, warmly enough, with the child "dozed off" (*STN*, 30) on his father's shoulder. What is suggested, perhaps, by the digression on the comedian, by the digression on the father's stories, by both digressions held in tandem, is the fragile artifice of the story, the deep needs served by the story, or both the story's fragile artifice and deep purpose. "We are, needless to say, in a skull" (*STN*, 38), says "The Calmative," however needlessly. But what skull? Whose skull? The narrator's? Beckett's? The reader's?

But even as it thus sabotages itself and ridicules its own making, "The Calmative," once it turns to making, is made more openly, more fully. Its lyric affirmations are less guarded, their celebrations less abashed. When the narrator, having reached the town and passed through it to the edge of the sea, is met there by a boy with a goat who offers him a sweet, he is "more and more moved since that is what I wanted" (*STN*, 33). The moment is presented in considerable detail, in a tone of undefended affirmation: "The sweets were stuck together and I had my work cut out to separate the top one, a green one, from the others, but he helped me and his hand brushed mine" (*STN*, 33). A green one, indeed. "The Calmative," as it adventures more persistently in these somehow opposite directions, is a more finished effort, more certain in the "fidelity to failure"[17] soon to be articulated as an aesthetic credo by its author, more assured in its possession of the means of defeat.

Following an initial, paragraph-long introduction of himself as a posthumous man—"I don't know when I died," he opens—whose consciousness persists in the grave ("my icy bed"), frightened by his body's decay ("the great red lapses of the heart, the tearings at the caecal walls"), the narrator moves on to "tell myself a story" (*STN*, 27). To escape his fright, "to try and calm myself" (*STN*, 27), he undertakes his narrative. The story is a "calmative," then, for its teller (who by electing a first-person mode becomes his own character), even as it speaks of other calmatives. The story tells of a journey, itself a calmative for the traveler, out and part way back, from and to "my distant refuge," to and from a nightmare "city" (*STN*, 28) complete with "Cyclopean and crenellated" (*STN*, 29) ramparts. The streets, mostly deserted, are crisscrossed by empty trams and buses. The few inhabitants encountered are grotesque characters, stars of bad dreams: "The only couple was two men grappling, their legs intertwined"

(*STN*, 38). An unlikely cyclist passes, "pedalling slowly in the middle of the street, reading a newspaper which he held with both hands spread open before his eyes" (*STN*, 38). A man in a church has "two burning eyes starting out of their sockets under a check cap" (*STN*, 36). A young woman, "perhaps of easy virtue, dishevelled and her dress in disarray, darted across the street like a rabbit" (*STN*, 38–39).

The exertions of this difficult, frightening journey, like the exertions of their narration, have as their end an escape from disquiet, the attainment of calm. What the struggling traveler wants of this odyssey, for motion for him is by no means easy, is company (as will be stressed later, Beckett's attraction to this word is also evident in the title of a 1980 work). What does anybody want, out of living, if living is what one wants, momentarily? Company. When dying is what one wants, and Beckett's characters mostly want dying, one wants peace, quiet, of body first and mind later; requisite for even the first of these preliminaries is solitude. Here, however, the stated goal is that of the living: to "achieve a little encounter that would calm me a little" (*STN*, 32).

He achieves several, and some of them do calm him. The one with the boy, for example, or a later one with a man who finally gives him a "phial" that may contain a calmative to beat all calmatives and before that suggests by his bizarre behavior—his voice murmurs "words so sweet" even as his "sinewy fingers" throttle the narrator's neck—the "devastating hope" (*STN*, 42) that he might be a loving killer. Still later, after the narrator has fallen, there is a "throng" that "paid no heed to me, though careful not to walk on me, a courtesy that must have touched me, it was what I had come out for" (*STN*, 45). He is moved; he is touched; he is not "returning empty-handed, not quite" (*STN*, 37)—hell, he may even have been given the means to kill himself. "It was well with me," he says as the considerate throng eddies around him, "sated with dark and calm, lying at the feet of mortals, fathom deep in the grey of dawn" (*STN*, 45).

But such moments of somber triumph belong, in these stories, to the narrator in his role as character. One character's pride in the mastery of begging's art, another's momentary attainment of calm, and a third's pleasure in lighting an oil lamp—these accomplishments are balanced, more than balanced, not only by complementary failures but also by inadequacies in their very telling, by endings that reject ending in the consideration of other beginnings, by descriptions that are abandoned in disgust, by assertions that are first qualified and then withdrawn, by moments of self-loathing that may extend to mockery of punctuation. When in "The End" the narrator berates himself for his laziness in shitting and pissing in the snug nest he has rigged in the abandoned boat—"I was so indolent and weak, so content deep down where I was"—he nevertheless admits it is a characteristic gesture. "To contrive a little kingdom," he says, "in the midst of the universal muck, then shit on it, ah that was me all over" (*STN*, 70). Nice pun. But surely, on the narrative level, the narrator does the same thing to the kingdom of words, to its contrived traditions, in a sentence such as, "Yes, yes, I said?" (*STN*, 43) from "The Calmative." Or perhaps this is a typo? But not with this writer.

Texts for Nothing

In *Texts for Nothing* this exposure of narrative fraud, the garrulous first-person voice's demonstration of its manifold incompetencies, assumes top billing. No more concise, straightforward confessions of failure or disinterest, like the "So much for that description" (*STN*, 12) of "The Expelled" or the "Enough about that" (*FL*, 31) of "First Love." Notice is served quickly, in the first sentence of Text 1: "Suddenly, no, at last, long last, I couldn't any more, I couldn't go on" (*STN*, 75). Revision is additive here, the rejected opening "Suddenly" is not blotted but instead revealed as unsuitable even while its continued presence undermines its successor, "at last," as arbitrary and itself soon to be modified. The sentence's end, "I couldn't go on," is similarly treated; it contains a negative assertion undermined by its bare existence (and by the tense of the verb) much as the opening's positive assertion is cancelled by the negative close on its heels. The result is a legible palimpsest that exposes the process of composition as do the chapter outlines included as summaries in *Mercier and Camier.* What is established by a sentence like this—and Beckett has by this time anchored his world in just such sentences, the *Three Novels* trilogy and *Waiting for Godot* being by the time of this writing already written—is a voice, unmistakable, strangely disembodied, sourceless and driven, persisting in despair as voice and voice alone.

In Text 1 that voice hears another voice, perhaps several, and addresses several props, two especially, a body and a head, but it stops short of asserting possession or identity: "I say to the body, Up with you now, and I can feel it struggling, like an old hack foundered in the street, struggling no more, struggling again, till it gives up" (*STN*, 75). A different tack is tried with the head: "I say to the head, Leave it alone, stay quiet, it stops breathing, then pants on worse than ever" (*STN*, 75). Two opposite orders, neither obeyed, despite efforts at obedience. Act, body is told, and body tries, twice, but gives up, does not act. Do not act, mind is told, and mind tries, tries to give up, strange attempt, surely, but gives up, acts. This voice, manipulating heads and bodies and their sometimes specified parts, presides over Text 1; and yet, speaking in a welter of pronouns, it insists on its impotence: "It's simple," he says (he is still male here, though by Text 3 gender will be rendered uncertain), "I can do nothing any more, that's what you think" (*STN*, 75).

Even the titles proclaim the fragmentary nature of the contents; these are not stories, like "The Expelled" or "The Calmative," but mere texts, and texts "for nothing" at that. "All mingles," the voice admits, "times and tenses," and then it adds that "I don't try to understand, I'll never try to understand any more" (*STN*, 78). But despite himself he does go on, "always muttering, the same old mutterings, the same old stories" (*STN*, 78). It is suggested, but only suggested, that the "stories" may be first heard, presumably from the other voice or voices, and then muttered. He is "all ears always, all ears for the old stories" (*STN*, 78). It is further suggested, once again, as in "The Calmative," and then explicitly in Text 2, that "perhaps we're in a head, it's as dark as in a head before the worms get at it, ivory dungeon" (*STN*, 82). Here, in Text 1, the first-person voice would appear to include the voice or voices, the body, the mind, and of course itself, in a single entity: "we're of one mind, all of one mind, always were, deep down" (*STN*, 77).

Through his speaking, scenes and characters, and with them stories, do take shape, however briefly. It is not until Text 4 that one voice manages wholly without a story, not until Text 10 that another manages without a proper name or place from beginning to end, and not until Text 13, the last, that the voice achieves a complete disembodiment. These gains, or losses, except for the last, because it is the last, are soon lost, or regained. But all three—scenes, characters, stories—are no more durable here than that initial "Suddenly" in Text 1, a stillborn word if there ever was one. When Mercier's thoughts, in *Mercier and Camier,* are described as "a dark torrent of brooding where past and future merged in a single flood and closed, over a present for ever absent,"[18] it seems clear that Mercier, given a voice and ordered to speak, given a pen and ordered to write, would be admirably qualified to undertake the *Texts for Nothing.*

The evanescent stories in Text 1 describe a familiar character, indigent, transient, prostrate on a rainy hilltop, "flat on my face on the dark earth sodden with the creeping saffron waters it slowly drinks" (*STN*, 76). He should have stayed home, of course: "All you had to do was stay at home" (*STN*, 76), says the voice he hears, or one of the voices, he can not be sure. But perhaps he could not be calm, staying at home, and so he ventures out, foolishly, in search of company. That happens in "The Calmative." Or perhaps he is evicted; there is a precedent for that, too. Now he is waiting for night, when the mist will clear, "I know my mist," and then he will be able to use the stars, "including the Bears, to guide me once again on my way" (*STN*, 78). But help comes sooner than the stars, in the form of a memory, one of the "old stories" (*STN*, 78), itself also familiar, the one first heard when "my father took me on his knee," about Joe Breem, or Breen, the lighthouse keeper's son. That story is a good one; it serves the man now as it once served the child, even though it is a memory now, a memory of a story, so that now "I was my father and I was my son, I asked myself questions and answered as best I could" (*STN*, 79).

Perhaps it was always a story; perhaps this father is the happy fiction of an unhappy son. Through all these removes, all the weavings and patchings of memory and fabulation, and despite the failures of both, which leave holes in its fabric, the story retains its power: "Joe jumped into the sea, that's all I remember, a knife between his teeth, did what was to be done and came back, that's all I remember this evening" (*STN*, 79). What matters, always, is the eager, not merely willing suspension of disbelief, the gullibility that calms and saves. "That's how I've held out till now," the voice says. "And this evening again it seems to be working," he continues, nearly done, only four lines to go, "I'm in my arms, I'm holding myself in my arms, without much tenderness, but faithfully, faithfully. Sleep now, as under that ancient lamp, all twined together, tired out with so much talking, so much listening, so much toil and play" (*STN*, 79). In the head, ascribing for now for the sake of peroration a head to the voice, father and son yet abide, as characters, fall asleep together in timeless and placeless mingling of times and tenses, tired out, the father with talk and toil, the son with listening and play, the voice with speaking their story, the head with being their home. And the ancient lamp, shedding its light on sleeping father and sleeping son and to the closed eyes lying in a trough in the rain, waiting for night—it is an oil lamp. Isn't it? Very likely.

Succeeding texts elaborate similar strategies. Text 2 manages brief vignettes about Mother Calvet the bag lady and Mr. Joly the bell ringer, the latter possesses "only one leg and a half" (*STN*, 83), and the former staggers through her nights with "her dog and her skeletal baby buggy," waving "a kind of trident" and "creaming off the garbage before the nightmen come" (*STN*, 81). Both are identified as coming from "above," where "the living find their ways," and the voice remembers moving among them, "between the cliffs and the sea" (*STN*, 81), returning "back to the den" (*STN*, 83) in a night filled with snow. "The day had not been fruitful," the voice admits, "as was only natural, considering the season, that of the very last leeks" (*STN*, 84). But even this "far memory" (*STN*, 84) has its consolations, for the voice no longer "there" (*STN*, 81), above, but "here," where "it's pure ache, pah you were saying that above and you a living mustard-plaster" (*STN*, 82). For the journey back to the den includes "a brief halt, opposite the lamplit window. A glow, red, afar, at night, in winter, that's worth having, that must have been worth having" (*STN*, 84).

Text 3, the longest of the lot at just over five pages, deploys other characters, a nurse named Bibby and a "crony, my own vintage" (*STN*, 87) named Vincent, but occupies itself more persistently with a meditation on the power of a first-person voice to "depart from here" by the bare act of saying. "I'll say I'm a body" (*STN*, 85), it says, and proceeds from there to a head, feet, and considerations of gender—"there has to be a man, or a woman, feel between your legs" (*STN*, 86)—thus picking up legs almost inadvertently, on the way, but after feet. That is part of the comedy, like God's order of creation in Genesis. From such preliminary flexing of narrative muscle it is an easy move to Bibby and Vincent, created at the drop of a word, and even they soon pale before more audacious creatures. "Just the head and the two legs, or one, in the middle, I'd go hopping," he says, he has decided to be a man. Or a male uniped. "Or just the head, nice and round, nice and smooth, no need of lineaments, I'd go rolling, downhill, almost a pure spirit, no, that wouldn't work, all is uphill from here" (*STN*, 89). Do we know where he is, then, after this possible allusive tip? At the center of the earth, crawling over Satan's body? It is possible; Text 9 ends with a more overt reference to Dante: the pilgrim's long climb to "see the stars again" (*STN*, 121).

But the end of Text 3, after this display of virtuosity, arrives not in the moment of attained calm, as its predecessors, but in the collapse of all these varied creatures and indeed their very ground. "I'm here," says the voice, "that's all I know, and that it's still not me, it's of that the best has to be made. There is no flesh anywhere, nor any way to die" (*STN*, 90). The voice, in its first-person placeless "here," can never be identified with any of its creatures, can never achieve a body to rest in or a story to die in, not even a story to end this text in calm with. It is enough, as *The Unnamable* knows, to make one "even regret being a man, under such conditions, that is to say a head abandoned to its ancient solitary resources" (*TN*, 361).

Text 4 employs these resources more carefully, no swagger here, issuing Bibbys and Vincents as if there were no tomorrow, no million tomorrows, to be gotten through somehow. It is puzzling, Text 4, in a new way; it seems to turn its gaze from third-person figments, though it names several in passing—"a vulgar Molloy, a common Malone" (*STN*, 92)—to examine and rebuke the first-person voice who "says this, saying it's me" (*STN*, 91). It is not; the first person apparently has no voice; it is always a "he" who "tells his story every five minutes, saying it's not his, there's cleverness for you" (*STN*, 92). The voiceless "I"—whose ruminations yet appear as words on the page, perhaps he is a mute "scribe" (*STN*, 95), such a being is mentioned in Text 5—resents with some heat the voice's baseless appropriations, even wishes "he would dignify me with the third person, like his other figments" (*STN*, 92). But no, "He has me say things saying it's not me, there's profundity for you, he has me who say nothing say it's not me" (*STN*, 92).

It is strange, all this, as bad as the sudden cabaret in the pasture earlier, perhaps worse, what with perspectives shifting; the "I" whose voice managed stories and reviewed memories is now reduced to a "he." Perhaps it is another link in a chain of narrators and figments; Vladimir imagines such a thing in *Waiting for Godot* when gazing at the sleeping Estragon he says, "At me too someone is looking, of me too someone is saying, He is sleeping, he knows nothing, let him sleep on" (*G*, 58b). He is right, too; he is in a theater, where the patrons in their seats are invited both to include themselves and to extend the chain. But then, just as one explicates, as best one can, as before one revised the pasture, the "he" disappears, as the cabaret earlier, "there is only me" (*STN*, 92), and Text 4 proceeds to its close in first person ease. "I have all I need to hand, for to do what, I don't know, all I have to do, there I am on my own again at last, what a relief that must be. Yes, there are moments, like this moment, when I seem almost restored to the feasible" (*STN*, 93–94).

It is embarrassing, somehow, to work out one's paltry explanations only to have their premises vanish, and when the embarrassment is recurrent, one naturally suspects a trap, a deliberate mockery of one's expertise. Beckett includes several such stunts in *Waiting for Godot*, as when Vladimir and Estragon base a lengthy discussion on the premise of Vladimir's greater weight only to realize they have no idea who is heavier, or when a consideration of why Lucky does not put down the bags is vitiated by their being put down. These instances add credibility to suspicion.

Text 5 presents the first person as a "clerk" or "scribe" entangled in a courtroom setting, "in the toils of that obscure assize where to be is to be guilty" (*STN*, 95). The voice is here more explicitly connected to a more or less regulation head subjected to visual as well as aural assault, plus scene of sorts to go with the babble: "That's where the court sits this evening, in the depths of that vaulty night, that's where I'm clerk and scribe, not understanding what I hear, not knowing what I write" (*STN*, 98). Escape from this "vault" is possible, momentarily, by means of stories enacted by figments, called "phantoms" here, who "issue from this imaginary head, mingle with air and earth," and then return, "come back and slip into the coffin, no bigger than a matchbox, it's they have taught me all I know, about things above" (*STN*, 99). The focus in Text 5, however, is not on such stories, or the phantoms who speak them and indeed, closing the solipsism, "speak to me of me, speak of a me," but on the talking head they inhabit and create, on its sense of being ensnared and subject to judgment, obliged to "record the doom, don the black cap and collapse in the dock" (*STN*, 98).

Text 6 shifts focus to the judges, or "keepers" (*STN*, 101), also imagined as "ghouls" and "male nurses" (*STN*, 102) (and as "demons" [*STN*, 119] in Text 9), who sometimes disappear, perhaps to "snatch a little rest and sleep before setting about me afresh" (*STN*, 101). These figures, in whatever visual guise, may embody the voices the narrator is obliged to hear and perhaps to repeat, as stories, as memories. Or they may not. Text 7 employs the word "pensum," for the first time in the *Texts for Nothing*, to describe the act of the "scribe" or "clerk" described in Text 5. He must keep speaking, keep writing, says Text 6, because the stories and memories have failed of their assignment and thus of their purpose—the assignment being, by means of words, to "get at me in the end" (*STN*, 102), and the purpose being that end itself, silence, the release from pensum, the death worthy of the term that apparently follows only on the completed assignment: "It's because I haven't hit on the right ones, the killers, haven't heaved them up from that heart-burning glut of words" (*STN*, 105). That is his life now, "this pell-mell babel of silence and words," if it is in fact "life still, a form of life, ordained to end" (*STN*, 104).

Both Text 6 and Text 7 include fragmentary stories, not the right ones, apparently, but "better than nothing," as Hamm asserts of his own story in *Endgame*, only to have Clov react with amazement, "Better than nothing! Is it possible?" (*E*, 59). Text 7 even briefly attempts a sort of Ur-character called X, a "paradigm of human kind, moving at will, complete with joys and sorrows, perhaps even a wife and brats, forbears most certainly, a carcass in God's image" (*STN*, 108). But this is a short-lived venture—X is soon dismissed as a "vile parrot" (*STN*, 108). Text 6 records a more sustained "whiff of life on earth" (*STN*, 104), seen behind the narrator's eyes; he has eyes in this text, "sealed this long time" (*STN*, 103). The scene reveals a boy of twelve staring into his father's shaving mirror, "in the bathroom, with its view of the sea, the lightships at night, the red harbor light" (*STN*, 103–4). This memory is complicated, however, immediately supplanted by other memories: "at the age of forty, for the mirror remained, my father went but the mirror remained, in which he had so greatly changed, my mother did her hair in it, with twitching hands, in another house, with no view of the sea, with a view of the mountains, if it was my mother" (*STN*, 104). He does not know, cannot be sure that these memories are his, that "I" is at last encountering "me," but "I must have believed in them an instant, believed it was me I saw there dimly" (*STN*, 103). But doubts are quick to surface. Even the mirror, the scene's durable element, assuring the linkage of these memories, is "double-faced, faithful and magnifying" (*STN*, 103).

Text 7, for its part, reverses the setting, provides a durable protagonist with mutable props. Here it is the "third class waiting-room of the South-Eastern Railway Terminus" (*STN*, 108) that greatly changes, falling into ruins while the passenger waits, "erect and rigid, hands on thighs, the tip of the ticket between finger and thumb, for a train that will never come" (*STN*, 110). Text 8 matches this grotesque with an ambulating costume (a blind, hard-of-hearing beggar's outfit, white stick, ear trumpet, bowler hat, "brown boots lacerated and gaping") equipped with a setting ("Place de la Republique, at pernod time") but suggests the absence of any protagonist at all: "These insignia, if I may so describe them, advance in concert, as though connected by the traditional human excipient" (*STN*, 114).

All these efforts, the boy, X, the railway passenger, the beggar, soon vanish, of course, like their predecessors, having served, perhaps, to occupy time, to allay momentarily the demands of obscure keepers, to move their teller as the narrator of "The Calmative" was moved by his encounters. When the beggar of Text 8 actually begs, for example, the moment of extending "my hand, or hat, without previous song, or any other form of concession to self-respect, at the terrace of a café, or in the mouth of the underground," is described as "affecting beyond all others" (*STN*, 115). At just this moment, the story collapses into its theme: "I would know it was not me, I would know I was here, begging in another dark, for another alm, that of being or of ceasing, better still, before having been" (*STN*, 115). Beckett's understanding of begging, of chains of beggars and Samaritans, is deepening here toward the succinct wisdom of *Embers*, where one realizes that one begs always "Of the poor."[19] In Text 8 the narrator is both beggar and philanthrope; as in Text 1 he is both father and son. They hold each other in their arms, in their heads, and the story delivers at its close its momentary calm, its succor recognized as vain: "And the hand old in vain would drop the mite and the old feet shuffle on, towards an even vainer death than no matter whose" (*STN*, 115).

These stories, all of them, take place, as Text 8 puts it, "in the mouth of the underground," yearning to be swallowed, as the beggar in the Place de la Republique yearns to be "deemed worthy of the adjacent Pere Lachaise" (*STN*, 115). Macmann, in *Malone Dies*, is roused even to lyric by such a prospect, addressing to his mistress Sucky Moll such effusions as, "To the lifelong promised land / Of the nearest cemetery / With his Sucky hand in hand / Love it is at last leads Hairy" (in *TN*, 262). But Text 9 complicates even this goal, raising as it does the possibility that life "above" is not something blessedly behind and only dimly remembered, but rather ahead, "here" being a kind of prior, embryonic state. Or perhaps it is both, the hair-raising possibility of resurrection, eternal return. If there was "a way out somewhere," says Text 9, "then all would be said, it would be the first step on the long travelable road, destination tomb . . . down the long tunnels at first, then under the mortal skies, through the days and nights" (*STN*, 118). It is a horrific myth of Er, this, without the menu of selection envisioned by Plato or the option of a sedentary choice recommended by Odysseus. Such considerations, here prolix, are those concentrated to an image in *Waiting for Godot*, in Vladimir's meditation by the sleeping Estragon: "Astride of a grave and a difficult birth. Down in the hole, lingeringly, the gravedigger puts on the forceps" (*G*, 58a). Beckett had already inverted these ruminations, too, in *Malone Dies*: "I am being given, if I may venture the expression, birth to into death, such is my impression. The feet are clear already, of the great cunt of existence. Favourable presentation I trust. My head will be the last to die" (in *TN*, 283). Earlier, the same novel speaks of being "far already from the world that parts at last its labia and lets me go" (*TN*, 189).

The concluding texts, beginning with Text 10, accomplish additional impoverishments, additional surrenders. Text 10 opens with "Give up," recognizing that this in itself is "nothing new" (*STN*, 123), but goes on to fill nearly three pages without so much as a moment's departure into a story or character from "above." Text 11 reverts briefly to visions of "a studious youth" (*STN*, 128) who in an instant, becomes "a snotty old nipper . . . in the two-stander urinal on the corner of the Rue d'Assas" (*STN*, 129), but Text 12 and Text 13 return to the empty felicities of Text 10. The first three texts, which at first reading seemed so bare, so paralyzed, now appear by contrast lavish in their attention to detail, crammed with characters and packed with action. Those texts had not just birds but curlews, not just stars but the Bears, not just bushes or brush but heath and ferns, not just trees but larches. Places and people abounded, well not quite abounded, but there was the Gobi, and Jellicoe, both in Text 3, and available for verification in any gazetteer. Even Text 8 is chock-full of such reassurances—Aristotle is there, along with Europe, Ireland, and the Bastille. But they are absent from the end, after the urinal, a last mention of Hail Marys, and the twice-uttered name of Jesus in Text 11. Is this an indication of pious purpose, that all direct reference to the recognizable earth closes on the name of Jesus? No.

The program for the close, this close anyway, is outlined in Text 10: "No, no souls, or bodies, or birth, or life, or death, you've got to go on without any of that junk" (*STN*, 125). Text 11 does not fully accomplish this emptying, nor does Text 12, although the latter is precise as to what is accomplished without it: "what's to be said of this latest other, with his babble of homeless mes and untenanted hims, this other without number or person whose abandoned being we haunt, nothing" (*STN*, 134). But Text 13, the last, features the voice totally disembodied, "a voice without a mouth, and somewhere a kind of hearing, something compelled to hear, and somewhere a hand, it calls that a hand, it wants to make a hand, or if not a hand something somewhere that can leave a trace" (*STN*, 137). There is almost a hand, just as there was almost something "Suddenly" at the beginning of Text 1. But there is no hand, "that's romancing, more romancing, there is nothing but a voice murmuring a trace" (*STN*, 137).

And this is how the *Texts for Nothing* end, as they began, in contradiction and admission of defeat, with "the impossible voice" in pursuit of "the unmakable being" (*STN*, 140), with the proclamation—no, that would be too grand for the "flurry of dust" (*STN*, 137) being chronicled here—with the tentative assertion of a conclusion undermined by its own end: "soon now, when all will be ended, all said, it says, it murmurs" (*STN*, 140).

From an Abandoned Work

Though later than the *Nouvelles* and the *Texts for Nothing*, *From an Abandoned Work* might serve admirably as an introduction to the latter in terms suggested by the former, so nicely does it combine their signatures in its eleven brief pages. Written in English in 1956, it introduces a recognizably earthly scene, establishes a conventional tense for its presentation, and presents a first-person narrator to carry on with the job. Very clean and efficient, no stutters, false starts, instant cancellations here: "Up bright and early that day, I was young then, feeling awful, and out, mother hanging out of the window in her nightdress weeping and waving."[20] It is all remembered, of course, "that day" simply "the day I have hit on to begin with, any other would have done as well, yes, on with it and out of my way and on to another," but that day was a good choice, or a lucky choice, filled with arresting details. The mother in the window, for instance: "The window-frame was green, pale, the house-wall grey and my mother white and so thin I could see past her (piercing sight I had then) into the dark of the room, and on that full the not long risen sun, and all small because of the distance, very pretty really the whole thing" (*SR*, 12).

This highlight is followed, amid frequent digressions, by "the only completely white horse I remember, what I believe the Germans call a Schimmel," seen in the distance accompanied by a boy, or perhaps "a small man or woman" (*SR*, 13). After this there is "nothing to add to this day with the white horse and white mother in the window," and the narrator moves on to a second day, "skipping hundreds and even thousands of days in a way I could not at the time, but had to get through somehow" (*SR*, 17). The second day provides a more striking story, but of course it is not told, just as "Draff" dismissed the rape and arson melodrama of the gardener and the servant girl. "What happens now," says the narrator, "is I was set on and pursued by a family or tribe, I do not know, of stoats, a most extraordinary thing, I think they were stoats" (*SR*, 17). (Stoats are ermines or weasels with black-tipped tails, the term applying especially to the animal in summer, when the fur is brown.) An extraordinary episode, indeed, but no description of this encounter follows, and in fact the stoats reappear only briefly, to be ignored again, at the fragment's close: "Is it the stoats now, no" (*SR*, 20).

Yet a third day follows; the "third day was the look I got from the roadman, suddenly I see that now, the ragged old brute bent double down in the ditch" (*SR*, 19). The roadman's name is Balfe: "I went in terror of him as a child. Now he is dead and I resemble him" (*SR*, 20). But no wonder this work was abandoned; things are getting out of control. Not only does the third day seem to precede the first and the second—there is no reason it should not perhaps—but the second suddenly returns, or perhaps the first—there is no way to be sure. These are all "old scenes" (*SR*, 20) anyway, "Now I am old and weak, in pain and weakness murmur why and pause, and the old thoughts well up in me and over into my voice" (*SR*, 15). The voice of the *Texts for Nothing* begins to take over, multiplying its pronouns, imagining another "then," not past but future, when there is "only a voice dreaming and droning on all around, that is something, the voice that once was in your mouth" (*SR*, 20).

But *From an Abandoned Work* no longer has its heart in such assaults on storytelling's conventions. They are recognized; they are noted, as the scribe from Text 5 says, but what is emphasized is the endurance of the old images, of the father and especially, here, of the mother, of animals and plants, the power they have to disquiet, but also to solace, the head or heart that is their home. What is it that oscillates like this, from compassion to vitriol? This narrator describes his mother in great detail, "the poor old thin lips pressed tight together and the body turned away and just the corners of the eyes on me," and with great compassion, "I heard her, talking to herself I suppose, or praying out loud, or reading out loud, or reciting her hymns, poor woman" (*SR*, 15). But then he turns immediately to savage rant: "Ah my father and mother, to think they are probably in paradise, they were so good. Let me go to hell, that's all I ask, and go on cursing them there, and them look down and hear me, that might take some of the shine off their bliss" (*SR*, 15–16).

What is it that can accomplish such a range of response? Love, isn't it? Love resisted in vain, as in "First Love." The word is recurrent in *From an Abandoned Work* applied to everything from words themselves to the act of lying face down, but applied at greatest length to the earth itself, in one of the author's most unabashedly lyric passages:

> Oh I know I too shall cease and be as when I was not yet, only all over instead of in store, that makes me happy, often now my murmur falters and dies and I weep for happiness as I go along and for love of this old earth that has carried me so long and whose uncomplainingness will soon be mine. Just under the surface I shall be, all together at first, then separate and drift, through all the earth and perhaps in the end through a cliff into the sea, something of me (*SR*, 17).

Shades of Whitman and the grass! Beckett frequently undermines this story, and other stories, by employing one term or phrase in two or more opposed contexts, as for example the word "then," which may refer either to time past or to time future, or both, or the phrase "out of my way," which is used first to refer to a detour—"no, I simply will not go out of my way, though I have never in my life been on my way anywhere" (*SR*, 11)—and later to refer to an obstacle—"yes, on with it and out of my way and on to another" (*SR*, 12). The word "enough" is one of Beckett's favorites; he even uses it as a title. It can refer to either a sufficiency or a surfeit. Here the story is abandoned, left unfinished, but not before escaping its own strictures, not before indulging its own nostalgias and rages with considerable abandon. Even that word in this story's title is resonant at the close.

Minima

Directing productions of *Waiting for Godot* in 1975, and again in 1984, Beckett made substantial alterations in his most famous play. At least one reader/spectator disapproved, seeing in the changes "an impoverishment of the original" amounting to "textual vandalism," but conceded that the changes offered not only a glimpse of "the vision Beckett now has of a greyer world," but "an incomparable barometer of the evolution of the Beckettian world view."[21] That evolution is no less clear in the short fiction, where a "greyer world" is increasingly present in the works of the 1960s. This may seem surprising, after the considerable grey evident in the *Texts for Nothing*, but even a short glance at *Imagination Dead Imagine* would likely convince most readers. The tendency already apparent in the 1950s in the *Texts for Nothing* and *From an Abandoned Work* toward brief pieces presented as fragments—what Murphy in reference to what a fastidious dachshund would not eat called "rejectamenta" (*M*, 102)—is accelerated in the work of the 1960s.

The works in question may be counted as seven: *All Strange Away, Imagination Dead Imagine, Enough, The Lost Ones, Ping, Lessness,* and *Fizzles. All Strange Away* and one *Fizzle* work ("Still") were done first in English; the others first appeared in French. Most commentators have treated *All Strange Away* as an early version of *Imagination Dead Imagine,* a view that apparently has the author's support. *Fizzles* consists of eight sections published in varying orders in different editions and written at times ranging from before *All Strange Away* to after *Lessness.* Given such complexities, so exasperating to the lover of sequence and its attendant orders, it seems best to respect the integrity of *Fizzles* (as published in the Grove Press American edition, since this seems to follow Beckett's instructions[22]), and treat it as the last of the sequence. *All Strange Away* is 27 pages in print; *Imagination Dead Imagine* fills only 4. This is typical, as it turns out, of Beckett's practice.[23] As early as 1931, in his critical study of Proust, he had, in the callow voice of oracle, articulated it as a matter of principle: "The artistic tendency is not expansive, but a contraction" (*P*, 47).

47

All Strange Away

What is most obviously new here is setting. The opening assertion of
the impossible accomplished—"Imagination dead imagine"—may by
this point no longer seem surprising, but it is shortly followed by the
explicit rejection of that by now standard itinerary, the ejection/depar-
ture from home or haven of a more or less vagrant narrator/protagonist,
succeeded by his wanderings, mental and physical, in search of renewed stasis, mental and physical. "Out of the door and down the road
in the old hat and coat like after the war, no not that again."[24] Instead,
as if attempting a more detailed portrait of the posthumous (or pre-
natal) world of the *Texts for Nothing*, a very different scene is presented:
"Five foot square, six high, no way in, none out, try for him there." A
cavalier move, this one, a spatial equivalent of the temporal "Suddenly, no, at last" (*STN*, 75) of Text 1, and rich in permutative ore.
Confinement replaces ejection; instead of a setting that expands, leaving newly homeless protagonists forever lifting their eyes to the sky,
whence cometh most often rain, and attempting to find their way, any
way, by means of stars, expecially the Bears, attention here turns to
settings that contract, imprison, immure. In *All Strange Away* several
such changes are made. First the cube shrinks—"Tighten it round
him, three foot square, five high" (*R*, 42). Then it shrinks again:
"down two foot, perfect cube now, three foot every way, always was"
(*R*, 47). Next comes a more spectacular remodeling; the cube gives
way to a "rotunda three foot diameter eighteen inches high supporting
a dome semicircular in section" (*R*, 54). After one last change, the
rotunda shrinking to "two foot diameter and two from ground to verge"
(*R*, 55), stability reigns for the last ten pages of the story. Stability of
setting, that is, for other instabilities have been present from the beginning, and yet abide. The inhabitant, for example, is male then female, is seated on a stool then standing then lying, is facing women's
faces, then naked bodies, female then male, on the walls, is clad in a
black bag then a shroud, then nothing, is clasping a grey rubber bulb
or ball then nothing, is murmuring quite an extensive repertoire—
"Mother, Mother in heaven, Mother of God, God in heaven, combi-
nations with Christ and Jesus, other proper names in great numbers say
of loved ones for the most part and cherished haunts" (*R*, 51)—then
murmuring nothing but "Fancy dead" (*R*, 63). Revisions like these,
comprising almost the entire piece, proceed in accordance with an explicit principle of need—"Imagine what needed, no more, any given

moment" (*R*, 40)—and seek in vain a stability envisioned in the title. All strange away—away with everything strange, that is, everything concocted by imagination, that fertile deceiver. Prune it, this is the imperative, down to "what needed, no more" so that "little by little all strange away" (*R*, 57).

But it is a doomed project; even the death of imagination must itself be imagined, and even the title phrase can assert the omnipresence of strangeness as well as its elimination. All strange away—everything is strange, that is, and there is no recourse but flight. Any work that takes on the domestication of the strange as its goal must always be an abandoned work, left derelict in a riot of proliferating visions and revisions, all of them strange. What is left is the old solace, "no more," the momentary calm, which was attained before with the help of the "old stories," like the one about Joe Breem in Text 1, or the image of "the lamplit window" that "must have been worth having" (*STN*, 84) in Text 2. Here what is left is one memory "of past felicity" (*R*, 60) mentioned four times in the final five pages, a "faint memory of a lying side by side" (*R*, 64). That is still present, still a "sop to mind" (*R*, 65) at the end, long after imagination and even fancy have been several times pronounced dead. The final sounds, here, are the "black vowel a" (*R*, 64) aspirated to a "faint sighing sound for tremor of sorrow at faint memory of a lying side by side and fancy murmured dead" (*R*, 65). It is all very strange, presented in a one-paragraph rush, all very moving, and it will not go away.

Imagination Dead Imagine

"No trace of life anywhere, you say, pah, no difficulty there"—this immediately cancelled opening assertion is by now something of an oblique signature for Beckett, and the tone of scoffing confidence is very shortly justified (*SR*, 35). There are, soon enough, "a thousand little signs" (*SR*, 38) of animation, carefully and tersely noted. Only by comparison with a piece as compressed as *Imagination Dead Imagine* could *All Strange Away* strike readers as diffuse, "shapeless and prolix."[25] In its four pages, the later story examines the "rotunda" of the earlier piece. There have been changes. Where Emma, the feminine phase of the rotunda's inhabitant in *All Strange Away*, was alone and able to "writhe," turning from left side to right side and moving from one "hemicycle" (*R*, 61) to the other as she did so, the unnamed

"white body of a woman" in *Imagination Dead Imagine* is both immo-
bilized and provided with a "partner" (*SR*, 37), also unnamed.

Two people, then, in a place, a severe and turbulent place where all
reference to a familiar earth, "islands, waters, azure, verdure," is omitted at the outset, where light's "white shine" is yoked to heat "hot but
not burning to the touch," while black dark keeps company with minimum temperature, "say freezing-point" (*SR*, 35). This place has
seemed, to critic upon critic, to be a skull, another skull, to go with
skulls mentioned earlier, in Text 2, for example, with its "ivory dungeon" (*STN*, 82), or with Malone's suspicion that these "eight, no six,
these six planes that enclose me are of solid bone" (*TN*, 221).

The narrator's examination of this scene, of its stilled though sen-
tient denizens, is conducted with a great show of precision, with scrupulous objectivity. The rotunda, for example: "Diameter three feet,
three feet from ground to summit of the vault. Two diameters at right
angles AB CD divide the white ground into two semicircles ACB BDA"
(*SR*, 35). The inhabitants: "Similarly inscribed in the other semicircle,
against the wall his head at A, his arse at B, his knees between A and
D, his feet between D and B, the partner. On their right sides therefore both and back to back head to arse" (*SR*, 37). Sound tests are also
conducted, and vital signs are noted.

The rotunda, when rapped, gives back a "ring as in the imagination
the ring of bone" (*SR*, 35). The figures are alive—"Hold a mirror to
their lips, it mists"—and not sleeping, for their left eyes "at incalcu-
lable intervals suddenly open wide and gaze in unblinking exposure
long beyond what is humanly possible" (*SR*, 37). They also "murmur
ah, no more, in this silence" (*SR*, 38). The variations of temperature
and light are also described in detail, the most common being an un-
broken 20-second transit from maximum heat and light to pitch black
and freezing, or the reverse.

But sometimes, and this is also very common, there are pauses between these poles, attended by vibrations, while at still other times
such pauses are ended not by resumptions but by reversals. "It is possible too, experience shows, for rise and fall to stop short at any point
and mark a pause, more or less long, before resuming, or reversing, the
rise and fall to stop short at any point and mark a pause, more or less
long, before resuming, or reversing, the rise now fall, the fall rise, these
in their turn to be completed, or to stop short and mark a pause, more
or less long, before resuming, or again reversing, and so on" (*SR*, 36).
There is, in the cataloging of these movements and their end points,

50

the usual pronounced bias in favor of the moments of stasis, of white or black, hot or cold, over the moments in transit, either in motion or at rest. In the piece's most comforting line, and poor comfort it is, the reader is told that "whatever its uncertainties the return sooner or later to a temporary calm seems assured, for the moment, in the black dark or the great whiteness, with attendant temperature, world still proof against enduring tumult" (*SR*, 36–37). The end points offer "temporary calm" (*SR*, 36), called in another place "lulls" (*SR*, 37) in contrast to the "feverish greys" (*SR*, 36) of the intermediate stages.

What occurs, of course, as the lineaments of this hellish scene emerge ever more clearly from the painstaking description, is that the description itself, with its tone of precise neutrality, is rendered ever more inappropriate. It becomes recognizable as the monstrous voice of a "science" run amok. Consider, for example, the following "experiment," undertaken at Dachau "to find a way for reviving aviators who had fallen into the ocean": "The subject was placed in ice-cold water and kept there until he was unconscious. Blood was taken from his neck and tested each time his body temperature dropped one degree. The drop was determined by a rectal thermometer. Urine was also periodically tested. Some men lasted as long as 24 to 36 hours. The lowest body temperature reached was 19 degrees C., but most men died at 25 degrees C., or 26 degrees C."[26]

This voice, surprisingly enough, is available not only to the scientists but also to their subjects, to whom it seems to offer something of an escape. Where the big picture is too appalling to face, one may concentrate on details. Consider, for example, this description of the infamous Black Hole of Calcutta, given from inside the bars:

> Figure to yourself, my friend, if possible, the situation of a hundred and forty-six wretches, exhausted by continual fatigue and action, crammed together in a cube of eighteen feet, in a close sultry night, in Bengal, shut up to the eastward and southward (the only quarters from whence air could reach us) by dead walls, open only to the westward by two windows, strongly barred with iron, from which we could receive scarce any the least circulation of fresh air.[27]

Beckett's story uses such tones from both perspectives. At first the woman and her "partner" are treated with clinical detachment, described as "Neither fat nor thin, big nor small, the bodies seem whole and in fairly good condition, to judge by the surfaces exposed to view.

The faces too, assuming the two sides of a piece, seem to want nothing essential" (*SR* 37–38). The whole point, of course, is that this sort of analysis is incapable of approaching anything "essential," much as a physician evaluating the condition of slaves on an auction block is prevented by the nature of the situation and the interests of his employers from anything like a meaningful assessment of "health."

In the world imagined by *Imagination Dead Imagine*, such detachment can only be comic in the darkest sense. And soon enough this tone is intruded upon, following the description of the murmured "ah" from the woman or the partner; the reporting onlooker "at the same instant" suddenly becomes the subject of description, has noted in his "eye of prey" an "infinitesimal shudder instantaneously suppressed" (*SR*, 38). The story ends then, in the collapse of distance, in the disappearance of the rotunda and its residents, the imagination's "little fabric" (*SR*, 35, 37) and the company it provided. That company, now gone, is treated with an open empathy—"no question now of ever finding again that white speck lost in whiteness, to see if they still lie in the stress of that storm, or of a worse storm, or in the black dark for good, or the great whiteness unchanging, and if not what they are doing" (*SR*, 38).

Enough

Enough is a wonderful story in Beckett's career, if only for the trouble it has brought to the posse of critics eager for the author to conform to an agenda of their liking, some program of formal experimentation, refreshingly linear and exhibiting such comforts as development and progress. *Enough* has done plenty, slight as it is, running to only seven pages, to discomfit such taxonomists. With its narrator "upright in the macrocosm, not yet reduced to crawling in the mud," it "backtracks to a world before *How It Is*," according to one reader; others see a similar retrogression in the utilization of paragraphs and a first-person narrator.[28] Still others, who absolve the author of such relapses, have stressed stylistic innovations that lead to more obviously original subsequent work, locating in this story the discovery of "the prose style that breaks decisively with what has gone before, the blend of passion and blandness, straightforwardness and obscurity, that is the hallmark of the comma-less writings of the late 'sixties and early 'seventies" (Knowlson and Pilling, 150).

Amid this welter of critical perplexities are some issues that seem forced, as if critics could suffer from such a thing as a shortage of perplexities. Considerable ink, for example, has been spilled in noting the indeterminate gender of the narrator. Beckett, scholarship has determined, was careful at one point to replace (in the original French) a phrase indicating a masculine narrator with a neutral participle. The text is open, of course, to varied interpretation and will be understood here as endorsing exactly such variety. The narrator could be a hermaphrodite, or even a mandrill. But I choose a human female—this seems least forced in a story entirely devoted to the chronicling of a twosome's long association that ends with reference to "my old breasts" reliving the "feel" of "his old hand" (*SR*, 31).

The voice of a female narrator, then, is captured in coherent sentences and paragraphs by "the pen. . . . I don't see it but I hear it there behind me" (*SR*, 25). Her story is of a paired wandering, her association beginning when she was "emerging from childhood" (*SR*, 26) with an old man who resembled "a tired old ape" (*SR*, 27), told through to its end when "he told me to leave him" (*SR*, 25). Within this interval is another, sharing the close but not the opening, which begins when "alluding for the first time to his infirmity he said he thought it had reached its peak" (*SR*, 28) and ends again with "the day of my supposed disgrace" (*SR*, 29). It is this time, the part of the then future that "we were able to make past of together" (*SR*, 28) that must now prove sufficient, be "enough," a comfort and calmative for the lonely survivor. "It is then I shall have lived then or never" (*SR*, 29), she says.

The duration of this central interval is uncertain, of course, but it is estimated to be "Ten years at the very least" (*SR*, 29). The couple spends their time wandering, her left hand in his right, both hands usually but not always gloved, "we must have covered several times the equivalent of the terrestrial equator" (*SR*, 27). The time is filled with various enjoyments, including climbing ("He loved to climb and therefore I too" [*SR*, 29]), mathematics ("We took flight in arithmetic. What mental calculations bent double hand in hand!" [*SR*, 27]), and stargazing, accomplished only with the aid of a mirror on account of "his" bowed posture. This "long outing was my life" (*SR*, 28) affirms the narrator. After the first paragraph, an introduction reluctantly devoted to matters of "art and craft," the narration turns immediately to its central couple, outlining first the conditions of their compatibility, second the circumstances of their parting, and third those of their join-ing. "I did all he desired," she begins. "I desired it too. For him. Whenever he desired something so did I" (*SR*, 25). This declarative reporting modulates by midparagraph to the tentative assertion so char-acteristic of Beckett's speakers, as much an expression of hope as the staking of a claim: "We must have had the same satisfactions. The same needs and the same satisfactions" (*SR*, 25).

The male partner, ruin that he is, is another Belacqua figure—his posture and association with climbing clearly echo references to Belac-qua in *Murphy* and *More Pricks than Kicks*—and the scene of their asso-ciation is a purgatory stripped of direction.[29] If Dante's Earthly Paradise seems at times nearly present, in the repeated references to flowers, the mild, windless weather, "As if the earth had come to rest in spring" (*SR*, 30), there nevertheless seems to be no hint of a para-dise ahead: "The crest once reached alas the going down again" (*SR*, 29). The same curve describes the larger motions, giving the whole piece a tone of nostalgia in the root sense. The pain of return, based on the impossibility of return. Why impossible? Because the place has changed, and with it the people, and with these changes the subject who cherished them. Beckett's discussion, in *Proust*, of the narrator's visit to his grandmother, is a vivid illustration. The narrator, appalled, realizes that "the cherished familiar of his mind," that is, the grand-mother of yesterday, "is dead, long since, and many times," and that the "mad old woman" before him is "a stranger whom he has never seen" (*P*, 15). The conclusion is general: "the only true Paradise is the Paradise that has been lost" (*P*, 14).

In *Enough*, then, the togetherness once reached, alas the separation again. "It's a rare thing," says Clov, "not to have been bonny—once" (*E*, 42). And memory of bonny times, after bonny times are over, well, there are differing opinions. Vladimir thinks they must be "un-pleasant" (*G*, 55b); Winnie, in *Happy Days*, has nothing but desperate praise for her "happy memories."[30] In *Enough* the bonny times are just that—sufficient—serving now as flowers served before, as calmatives. Flowers and the memory of flowers, flowers then trod upon and eaten, flowers now remembered, with this bouquet the story ends: "We lived on flowers. . . . They had on the whole a calming action. We were on the whole calm. . . . Now I'll wipe out everything but the flowers. . . . Nothing but the two of us dragging through the flowers. Enough my old breasts feel his old hand" (*SR*, 31).

The Lost Ones

By 1971–72, when *Le Depeupleur/The Lost Ones* appeared, in the original French and English translation, readers accustomed to Beckett's minimalist mode were prepared to see its 57 pages as something like sustained narrative. The tone is that of *Imagination Dead Imagine*—scrupulous objectivity and clinical detachment are here vaguely anthropological, devoted to the observation and description of not just one pair but a whole culture of sorts. Two hundred "bodies," more or less, are situated in a "flattened cylinder fifty metres round and eighteen high for the sake of harmony."[31] They see it as a prison and struggle in various ways with their incarceration. Some, called "amateurs of myth" (*LO*, 21), believe in the existence of "a way out," though these believers divide into two camps over the issue of the exit's location, while others are no longer "loyal to that old belief" (*LO*, 18).

The major divisions among the cylinder's inhabitants, four in number, are measured according to visible activity, outward physical motion being taken as indicating inward will. A hierarchy of striving results: "Firstly, those perpetually in motion. Secondly, those who sometimes pause. Thirdly those who short of being driven off never stir. . . . Fourthly those who do not search" (*LO*, 13–14). Figures in the third group are often referred to as "the sedentary"; those in the fourth are "the vanquished." All is governed by a sort of fitful entropy, so that "in the beginning then unthinkable as the end all roamed without respite" (*LO*, 34). The unthinkable end is of course thought. In the story's fifteenth and final section, none roam at all, and all but one "last body of all" (*LO*, 60) are vanquished. This one too then "finds at last his place and pose whereupon dark descends and at the same instant the temperature comes to rest not far from the freezing point" (*LO*, 62).

In between is all the trouble, the elaborate rules controlling movement on the cylinder's floor, the "climber's code" (*LO*, 27) governing the use of the 15 ladders and the occupation of the "score of niches some connected by tunnels," which are "disposed quincuncially for the sake of harmony" (*LO*, 17) in the upper half of the wall. All these are fulsomely recorded, together with equally precise environmental observations. The text reads like a description of an exotic tribe by a diligent ethnographer given at times to quaint rotundities of style and occasional patronizing compliments for the system's adequacy in meeting the needs of its citizens. Describing a niche occupant who has overstayed his allotted time and thus lost control of the ladder that conveyed him to the head of the queue below, the narrator notes his "situation" as "delicate indeed" since it "seems to exclude a priori his ever returning to the ground" (*LO*, 23). But no: "Happily sooner or later he succeeds in doing so thanks to a further provision giving priority at all times to descent over ascent. He has therefore merely to watch at the mouth of his niche for a ladder to present itself and immediately start down quite easy in his mind knowing full well that whoever below is on the point of mounting if not already on his way up will give way in his favour" (*LO*, 23–24).

An imposing constellation of reassurances, certainly, leading their bearer inexorably to a clinching banality: "So all is for the best" (*LO*, 42). Such a conclusion, of course, is finally unconvincing; its rhetorical blandishments are undermined at every point by paradox ("Paradoxically the sedentary are those whose acts of violence most disrupt the cylinder's quiet" [*LO*, 14]), oxymoron ("making unmakable love" [*LO*, 37], "irregular quincunxes" [*LO*, 11]), and open confession ("All has not been told and never shall be" [*LO*, 51]). For the anthropologist/ narrator, no less than for the "little people of searchers" (*LO*, 63) he describes, it must at last be acknowledged that "in this old abode all is not yet quite for the best" (*LO*, 61). They remain lost ones together, searching and striving, looking for "a way out" (*LO*, 18), and if their story ends with the narrator going "on infinitely" to think at last "the unthinkable end" (*LO*, 60) just as the little people make "unmakable love" (*LO*), 37), there inheres in their efforts "the slight taint of pathos" (*LO*, 39), as always, despite dispassion's rigors. *The Lost Ones* may be Beckett's deepest homage to Dante, his most loved master, whose bust he had displayed in his room from boyhood. It is a succinct *Inferno*, finally, complete with overt bows ("a flue at the end of which the sun and other stars would still be shining" [*LO*, 18]), told almost apologetically ("So much roughly speaking" [*LO*, 16]) by an "amateur of myth" much less convinced than his predecessors, the whole fabric of his envisioned cylinder lasting only so long as "this notion is maintained" (*LO*, 63).

Ping

If *Enough*, in its apparent retrogression, has been the despair of Beckett's academic handlers, *Ping*, with its formal rigor and amply documented history of revision, has been one of their great delights. First published in French (as *Bing*) in 1966 and translated into English in 1967, *Ping* in 1970 became the first of Beckett's works to be made widely available in "all ten typescript drafts, . . . covering its complex and changing development from first conception to final copy dispatched to the printer."[32] Twenty years later it remains one of its author's most minutely examined works. Commentators have counted this 1,030-word work's sentences (69) and the number of words in its vocabulary (120). Certain terms have been judged as keys owing to their frequency ("meaning," for example, occurs eight times, and "perhaps," eleven times) or their rarity ("nail," "hair," "scars," "flesh," and "torn," for example, occur only once each), and elaborate word frequency graphs have been published.[33]

"All known all white"—a serene and confident beginning, surely (*SR*, 41). But all is not known. The tortured qualifications ("almost never" is recurrent), the admissions of ignorance ("but that known not" [*SR*, 43]), the first "perhaps"—they surface soon enough. Nor is all white, despite the word's desperate reiteration—it is used 90 times, far more than any other. Soon enough there are grey, though "light grey almost white" (*SR*, 41), and blue, though "light blue almost white" (*SR*, 42), and before long there is also black and finally rose as well. The asserted purities, of sight, of sound, of time and place, of will and comprehension, are undermined, all of them, the white by colors, the silence by murmurs, present time and present space by memories of a "light time blue and white in the wind" (*SR*, 43).

The title term, "ping," occurring 34 times, is often associated with these pressing corruptions. They "impinge," that is the word, it means "encroach, infringe on." So, for example, "ping" is followed six times by "murmur," "murmurs," and "last murmur," nine times by "elsewhere," "fixed elsewhere," and "fixed last elsewhere," four times by "perhaps," three times by "of old," and once each by "a nature," "a meaning," and "image." Into the almost white almost silence of a dessicated present, then, these impingements bring murmured sounds, another time and place, even a hint of significance. Even here, in this emptiest and flattest of stories, there is a climax, a one-word, one-image intrusion, brief but insistent, of the old, unforgettable other. The word is "imploring"; the image is of the eye making the plea: "Ping perhaps not alone one second with image same time a little less dim eye black and white half closed long lashes imploring that much memory almost never" (*SR*, 43).

The word and the image recur at *Ping*'s close: "ping last murmur one second perhaps not alone eye unlustrous black and white half closed long lashes imploring ping silence ping over" (*SR*, 44). This is Beckett's uninsistent emphasis, sufficiently unobtrusive for critics stressing its centrality to be scoffed at as sentimentalists by other critics. But the sentimentalists are right. It is the old first love predicament again. Even when all is almost over, when all is "almost never" and "only just," the image of the other, like the sound of cries in "First Love," endures, continues to impinge. Not only is the only paradise the lost paradise—that sounds bad enough—but the lost paradise is present as lost, present in its broken pieces, shards now, cries and half-closed eyes imploring in vain. You can run, says "First Love," says *Ping*, but you cannot hide.

Lessness

Molloy, among other denizens of his creator's pages, loves to count and calculate. "Extraordinary how mathematics helps you to know yourself," he says, having just completed an analysis of his flatulence. He began in worry, "gas escapes from my fundament on the least pretext," but ended in calm, "I hardly fart at all, I never should have mentioned it" (*TN*, 30). That the computations are themselves flawed seems not to matter; in fact, Beckett and his creatures have long demonstrated a preference for issueless predicaments, answerless questions, asymptotic lines. "To know you are beyond knowing anything," says Molloy, "that is when peace enters in, to the soul of the incurious seeker. It is then the true division begins, of twenty-two by seven for example, and the pages fill with the true ciphers at last" (*TN*, 64).

If *Ping* is rich in such pleasures, providing hours of enjoyment for critics and their computers, *Lessness* is similarly gratifying. Where Beckett provided drafts of the former work, he supplied for *Lessness* something even better, given such tastes: a description of his method for composing it in deliberately random sentence order and paragraph structure. The 24-paragraph story consists of 60 different sentences, each used twice, and there are 12 paragraphs in each half of the story. Paragraph length and sentence order within paragraphs are arranged randomly. All this was accomplished by the creation of 6 groups of thematically related sentences, another list indicating the order of their selection, and a third list indicating the number of sentences in succeeding paragraphs. Critics have mostly been grateful, although there has been occasional dismay at "irrefutable evidence of this mechanical art."[34]

The true key, of course, is the sentences themselves, the phrases created not randomly but with their random combination foreseen. Beckett was very generous with his scholarly fans, as usual, but he has led them on a dreary chase as well, also as usual and no doubt with some grim pleasure, given the level of harassment he has tolerated. Writing to Alan Schneider long before, he had lamented the zeal for "headaches among the overtones" evident in critic and reviewer response to *Endgame*. Let them have them, he concluded, and "provide their own aspirin."[35] In the present instance, the zeal for quantification leads to something like "true ciphers, "away from the heart of the story. *Lessness*, it turns out, is easily recognizable, clearly a work of its author and not, for example, a work of William Burroughs, famed for his interest in stochastic maneuvers. *Lessness* may be in fact the most persistent of his many explorations of entropy, the end of entropy, the region or moment where less and less nudges down against zero.

The problem of ending, again, of being done, of falling silent, this is at the center here, again. Once more stasis seems established, at the beginning. Once more the world is reduced to "grey air timeless no sound. . . . Never but this changelessness" (*SR*, 47). But then, just on the heels of this flat claim, comes exactly that, in a cruel pun, a change to lessness, lessness changed to something else, entropy reversed, the sudden irruption of a person attached to a verb in the future tense: "He will curse God again as in the blessed days face to the open sky the passing deluge" (*SR*, 47, 51). Plenty of change there! An end to changelessness, then, an end to lessness.

And what is that end, another cruel reverse? But of course. Endlessness. The word occurs again and again, 24 times. The grey "little body heart beating only" (*SR*, 47, 50), its "genitals overrun arse a single block" (*SR*, 48, 51) is not only old but also new, an embryo rising like Christ from a tomb/womb, a grave itself now in ruins, its walls "split asunder over backwards" (*SR*, 48, 50). The image, and the cycle, should be familiar by now: birth into death into birth. Remember Vladimir: "Down in the hole, lingeringly, the grave-digger puts on the forceps" (*G*, 58a). Much the same movement, lessness to endlessness, the end of lessness, for the moment, is described in comic terms in *The Unnamable*, when Mahood is "coming to the end of a world tour" (*TN*, 317), moving in "a kind of inverted spiral" (*TN*, 316) toward the family home (a "rotunda," by the way, students of *All Strange Away* and *Imag-*

ination Dead Imagine, take note). He is able to imagine his approach, but not his arrival: "When I penetrate into that house, if I ever do, it will be to go on turning, faster and faster, more and more convulsive, like a constipated dog, or one suffering from worms, overturning the furniture, in the midst of my family all trying to embrace me at once, until by virtue of a supreme spasm I am catapulted in the opposite direction and gradually leave backwards, without having said good-evening" (*TN*, 321).

In *Lessness*, nobody is "catapulted" anywhere, but the change to "the opposite direction" occurs nevertheless, at the pace appropriate to this less frantic world. "He will stir in the sand" (*SR*, 47, 50), and from this merest shudder the whole multitudinous world will emerge again. "He will live again" (*SR*, 48, 50) with all his troubles renewed: "Old love new love as in the blessed days unhappiness will reign again" (*SR*, 48, 51). Here is the scenario dreaded by Hamm when Clov reports the existence of a flea, or perhaps a crab louse: "But humanity might start from there all over again! Catch him, for the love of God!" (*E*, 33). *Lessness*, broaching such despairs, unveils a language of nearly Biblical weight. "He will live again the space of a step it will be day and night over him the endlessness" (*SR*, 48, 50). And the evening and the morning were the first day. Or perhaps of heavier than Biblical weight. The last shall be first? The hoped for Apocalypse turns out to be Genesis in disguise? No wonder this story, like so many others, takes comfort in its own fictitiousness, its random qualities. If you thought God wrote such a story, you would be glad to learn He was a chimpanzee. "Figment dawn," the story ends, "dispeller of figments and the other called dusk" (*SR*, 51). Everywhere, everything figments, that is a relief. Clov's comfort, not knowing, is the best: "It's not certain" (*E*, 36).

Fizzles

Written between the late 1950s and the middle 1970s and first published together in 1976, the eight short works collected in *Fizzles* are even less related one to another than the components of *Texts for Nothing.* "For To End Yet Again," which opens the French and English editions, closes their American counterpart; "Still," alone in the collection in being written originally in English, stands second in the English edition, last in the French, and next to last in the American. "Afar a Bird," third in the American edition, is the only other text with a separate title there, although in the English version all items are given with titles, and what is simply "Fizzle 5" in the American version is "Se voir" in the French. The sequence of the American edition, apparently done at Beckett's direction, will be followed here.[36]

Fizzle 1 ("He Is Barehead" in the English edition) is written in the third person, unlike the first-person pieces that follow. It describes the movements of a figure in "vaguely prison garb" in a more than vaguely prison situation.[37] Moving in "gloom" (*F*, 9) along a path hemmed in by walls, he "does not grope his way, arms outstretched, hands agape," but moves bowed down, like the other "he" of *Enough*, with "his back humped, his head thrust forward, his eyes cast down" (*F*, 8). The resulting collisions with the walls draw blood, "but in no great quantity, the little wounds have time to close before being opened again, his pace is so slow" (*F*, 8).

The terrain on which he toils is a purgatorial slope, a rising climb interrupted by occasional sheer drops, but the air is that of hell, "so foul that only he seems fitted to survive it who never breathed the other, the true life-giving, or so long ago as to amount to never" (*F*, 13). He is only now constructing a history, "it is all still fragile," building on "a number of memories" (*F*, 12) that at their best restore "that first instant beyond which nothing, when he was already old, that is to say near death, and knew, though unable to recall having lived, what age and death are, with other momentous matters" (*F*, 12–13). Some of these latter are detailed, as for example "the sweetest wall lick" (*F*, 14) or "the loudest fall" (*F*, 13).

It is clear enough, even from this fizzled story, which ends on the promise of "fresh elements and motifs, such as these bones, of which more very shortly" (*F*, 15), that the toiling protagonist is living out the situation generalized in *Lessness*. He has lived already, so long ago as to amount to never, and he very likely once rejoiced at his decline and approaching death, assuming easily enough that he was ending, getting finished, that less and less would eventually subtract down to nothing, but now he is about to live again, the foul air of the present succeeded soon again by the true life-giving. "But the change from one to the other will no doubt be gentle, when the time comes, and gradual, as the man draws closer and closer to the open" (*F*, 13). In fact, there is always plenty of doubt in the worlds Beckett has mixed together from his favorite Dantesque elements, about the gentle and gradual nature of the change. If it is a birth, the gravedigger donning the forceps again, it will be anything but gentle. But "these bones," these dry bones, will live again, no matter how fine the dust into which they have crumbled. Or perhaps not Ezekiel's bones but Echo's are alluded to. It is possible—just four pages before the bones Fizzle 1 mentions "the echo" following upon sounds "of fall, a great drop dropping at last from a great height" (*F*, 11). And Echo, remember the suppressed final story of *More Pricks than Kicks*, the 1935 volume of poems, has appeared before. The bones, then, Echo's or Ezekiel's, will live again. There are few certainties in the world imagined here—its author has suggested to interviewers that "perhaps" is a key word in his work—but certitudes are not wholly absent. It is a matter of principle, after all. If nothing were certain one could be sure of uncertainty. As *Waiting for Godot* opens Estragon cannot identify his nocturnal assailants, or even be sure of himself, but of the assault itself he has no doubts: "Beat me? Certainly they beat me" (*G*, 7a). As Fizzle 1 closes many things are likewise uncertain, but one of these is not the absence of ending. There will be more, very shortly, just turn the page, more fizzling, more going on, more "fresh elements and motifs" (*F*, 15)—a nice joke, this, a bit of self-deprecation, here where the recycling of old elements and motifs is so obsessive. "I love the old questions," says Hamm (*E*, 38).

Fizzle 2 ("Horn Came Always" in England) actually does introduce an interrogative element new to the stories, though familiar enough from the drama and even the novels. The first-person narrator is visited, briefly but repeatedly and "always at night," by a secretary of sorts named Horn, who answers questions with the help of notes consulted by match light or "an electric torch" (*F*, 19). The relationship of the narrator to Horn is formal, elaborately correct: "He did not like one to interrupt him and I must confess I seldom had call to" (*F*, 20). Horn is most like Gaber, from *Molloy*, but the interrogative situation, which sometimes intensifies to inquisition, is prominent also in *Play*, where the inquisitor is a spotlight, and in *Eh Joe*, where it is a voice. Remember, too, the brief reference in *Imagination Dead Imagine* to the "eye of prey" (*R*, 38), which like the camera eye in *Film* pursues its subject with a prosecutor's zeal.

Equally elaborate, in the ceremonious voice employed by this narrator, is the interest in temporal matters: "But I speak now of five or six years ago. These allusions to now, to before and after, and all such yet to come, that we may feel ourselves in time" (*F*, 20). This Olympian note, with its hint of patronage, may remind Dante readers of Beatrice's address to the pilgrim in heaven, informing him that the discourse of herself and the other blessed is adjusted, diluted, and simplified to suit his less uplifted understanding.

Feeling ourselves in time, even if not exactly on earth, we may sense here, as in Fizzle 1, a "history" under construction, "still fragile" as it was there. Here, Horn's face, dimly lit by the "yellow glimmer" of the torch, is "more and more clearly the more it entered shadow, the one I remembered" (*F*, 21). The future, too, as in Fizzle 1, is projected as a time of return, a time for resuming previous activities. The narrator, for example, had once "pored over" his own face, "all down the years" (*F*, 19), but has since hidden it, even from himself, for "five or six years" (*F*, 20). "Now," he says, "I would resume that inspection, that it may be a lesson to me" (*F*, 19). Similarly, he is now rising from his bed again, in preparation for renewed travel: "I thought I had made my last journey, the one I must now try once more to elucidate, that it may be a lesson to me, the one from which it were better I had never returned. But the feeling gains on me that I must undertake another. So I have taken to getting up again and making a few steps in the room, holding on to the bars of the bed" (*F*, 21–22).

This narrator is another dead guy, isn't he, like the one crashing around in slow motion in Fizzle 1. This character is a Lazarus in training for Ulysses, taking up his bed and walking, soon to sail for the Antipodes, maybe, but this will do him no good either, most likely, since it is hinted that he is another fleeing lover as well, with bad memories, downright nightmares in his head. "And her gown that day?" (*F*, 20) he asks Horn, still reliving, still remembering, like Krapp of *Krapp's Last Tape* or Joe of *Eh Joe* or the narrator of "First Love" or the imprisoned "bare white body" (*SR*, 41) of *Ping*, the moment of failure, of the other's resultant grief, pain, death.

Fizzles 3 and 4 are much alike, very nearly simple variants one of the other. The author seems to have recognized this—Fizzle 3, "Afar a Bird," is unique in possessing no closing period, and both works share the tortured "I" versus "he" relationship familiar from the *Texts for Nothing* where "he" is the itinerant vagabond who lives and dies in the world "above," while "I" exists beneath, within, beyond, but somehow tied to "he," and more or less in control. "I'm still inside," says the voice of Fizzle 3, "the same, I'll put faces in his head, names, places, churn them all up together, all he needs to end" (*F*, 27). Like Text 4, however, this relationship can seem to shift, be turned inside out, the "he" now prior to "I," the "I" now produced by "he": "it was he had a life, I didn't have a life, a life not worth having, because of me, it's impossible I should have a mind and I have one, someone divines me, divines us, that's what he's come to, come to in the end, I see him in my mind, there divining us" (*F*, 26).

Most persistent in these two pieces, however, are the echoes from *From an Abandoned Work*. Not only does the frightening roadman Balfe reappear to be confused with "his father," but the earlier story's meditation on worms and its emphasis on love are also reiterated. "He" is, of course, another one who loves, who cannot not love, no matter how hard he tries. Among the listed items promised by "I" as food for "he" in his need to end is "an old curdog, a mangy old curdog, that he may love again, lose again" (*F*, 27). The dog is from *Molloy*; the love, the lost love, is from everything. Beneath, within, abiding through all the complexities of formal procedure, the suppressions of punctuation and permutations of syntax, the "I" lurking in "he," is this damning drive, unquenchable, to love somebody, something, anything, just long enough to harm it, maim it, cause it pain.

With Fizzle 5 the suggestions of other work shift forward to *The Lost Ones* and *Ping*, both of which are more successful. "Closed place," it begins, and continues to describe not an "I" or a "he" in their intimate combat but "millions" in a central "arena" (*F*, 37) or the "bed" (*F*, 38) of a "ditch" (*F*, 37). Between these two is a narrow "track" of "dead leaves" (*F*, 38) where "no two ever meet" (*F*, 39). Entropy reigns again, with dark squares in the ditch now outnumbering bright ones "by far," even though "In the beginning it was all bright" (*F*, 38). Future time and other place are suggested by a single reference to "beldam nature" (*F*, 38). Fizzle 5, finally, fizzles with less pop than the others. It is the dud of the lot, like "The Smeraldina's Billet Doux" in *More Pricks than Kicks*.

Fizzle 6 is even briefer, the briefest of the lot, but unlike Fizzle 5 it runs its little course with considerable zest. Opening in direct address to the earth, in celebration again of the old promise, from "First Love," of the "many graves in her giving, for the living" (*FL*, 35), the narrator first claims such intimacy as his due ("You'll be on me, it will be you, it will be me, it will be us" [*FL*, 43]), only to recognize that this insistence fails to serve his purpose, to achieve an end. Not even what Dan Rooney, in the radio play *All That Fall*, calls "fully certified death" (*KLT*, 79), not even the burial following upon such certification—not even these signal occasions on life's way can guarantee an end to that way. Here the suggestions of "a cockchafer year" (*F*, 43) are brought forward, "Three years in the earth, those the moles don't get, then guzzle, guzzle, ten days long" (*F*, 44). Then "next year there won't be any, nor the year after" (*F*, 43). A cycle, again, eternal return, "a veritable calvary, with no limit to its stations" (*TN*, 78). (Cockchafers are European beetles.)

This narrator, after watching the cockchafers' evening flight, stands "ashamed" by his window in the dusk, looking at the sky. But there is no calm, for him, in the close of day, the fall of light. The story ends instead in "gasps and spasms" of unquenchable memories; the skies themselves "turn to faces, agonies, loves, the different loves, happiness too, yes, there was that too, unhappily" (*F*, 44). It is lovely, another moment of undefended lyric, and it is terrible in its isolation: "Moments of life, of mine too, among others, no denying, all said and done. Happiness, what happiness, but what deaths, what loves, I knew at the time, it was too late then. Ah to love at your last and see them at theirs, the last minute loved ones, and be happy, why ah, uncalled for" (*F*, 44). Why "ah uncalled for"? Because no ah when called for, in those "moments of life" now lost and unforgettable. Why ashamed? Because no ah when called for, when cried for, when implored. Perhaps.

"For years I thought they would cease," says the narrator of "First Love," speaking of Lulu's cries. "Now I don't think so any more" (*FL*, 36). Fizzle 6 never mentions cessation. The faces, the agonies, the loves, the moments of life, they all endure, invade even the shapes of the evening sky. The story ends in enduring: "No but now, now, simply stay still, standing before a window" (*F*, 44).

Standing still before a window—this is an easy transition to Fizzle 7, "Still," the one done first in English. A sunset and several windows figure prominently. But what is most striking in "Still" is the painstaking description of external setting and movement in a story remarkable for its stark setting and absence of movement. Here is the plot: a man (or a woman) sits in a chair by a window, occasionally opening and closing his/her eyes; eventually the right hand is lifted "not midway to the head but almost there" and the head in turn "moves from its place forward and down" to meet the "ready fingers" and by its weight pushes the elbow back to the chair's armrest. That's it; "the hours pass" and "night wears on" (*F*, 50) without additional action.

Beckett does manage, however, almost in the very act of stressing external stasis, to hint at internal agitation. The hand over the face, for example, may suggest that "even in the dark eyes closed not enough and perhaps even more than ever necessary against that no such thing the further shelter of the hand" (*F*, 50–51). "Still" also demonstrates again a lesson familiar since *Watt*: the inevitable failure of exactitude even in a purely external description. Hugh Kenner has written of that novel's demonstration in "gentle scrupulous sentences" of "the incapacity of language . . . to locate with finality any datum, or define with assurance any relation."[38] Here, despite the recurrence of the title word (24 times), it is eventually admitted (3 times) that things are "not still at all" (*F*, 48, 49). The seated body, in fact, is "trembling all over" (*F*, 48).

Another tough night in the Beckett country, fraught with nightmare, faces, agonies, imploring eyes, the cries of childbirth. "Be again, be again," says Krapp, who has his own obsessive memories, notably the memory of a lost love that will not go away. He is making his last tape, he says, again, but he should know better. "All that old misery," he calls it. But what he describes is far from miserable: "Be again in the dingle on a Christmas Eve, gathering holly, the red-berried. (*Pause.*) Be again on Croghan on a Sunday morning, in the haze, with the bitch, stop and listen to the bells" (*KLT*, 26). This is happiness; those were happy moments, no denying that, unhappily. They remain, present as lost, like the memories of the "girl in a shabby green coat, on a railway-station platform" or the particular plague of this birthday evening, the memory of the bright day on the "upper lake," the day of agreed parting—"I said I thought it was hopeless and no good going on, and she agreed" (*KLT*, 22). The play ends with that memory, vivid after thirty years, repeated: "We drifted in among the flags and stuck. The way they went down, sighing, before the stem! (*Pause.*) I lay down across her with my face in her breasts and my hand on her. We lay there without moving. But under us all moved and moved us, gently, up and down, and from side to side" (*KLT*, 27). "Still" is a sparer piece, offering now's agitations without then's enduring causes. It is Krapp without his tapes; now they play only in his head.

Fizzle 8, "For To End Yet Again," was written, like "Still," in the 1970s, not only later than the other Fizzles but later than *Lessness, Ping, The Lost Ones*, and the other "abandoned" and "residual" works of the 1960s. At six pages, it is the second longest in the volume (after Fizzle 1), and its title suggests its central concerns, old central concerns, quite adequately. It is endgame again, another botched ending again. Although it closes the American edition, it opens the French and English, as if beginnings and endings are confused, and they are. The first sentence says it all, beginning with ending and ending with beginning:

"For to end yet again skull alone in a dark place pent bowed on a board to begin" (*F,* 55). The last sentence says it all again, speaking hopelessly of "another end" and constructing something like a future perfect conditional to imagine "a last end if ever there had to be another absolutely had to be" (*F,* 61). The title phrase, in fact, will be used again, in another, later end, in *Ill Seen Ill Said.* But all this is logical after all, even necessary, perhaps; you have to begin in order to end. Or is this a mistake, a truly fundamental mistake, as any ordinary intelligence might notice? What you must do in order to end is not begin.

The "skull alone" soon "makes to glimmer again in lieu of going out" (*F,* 55), and by virtue of this glimmering is of course, no longer alone. First there is "a leaden dawn" in whose lingering gray appears "erect amidst his ruins the expelled" (*F,* 56). So much for setting and character. Now for action: "First change of all in the end a fragment comes away and falls" (*F,* 56). But already there are problems with this story. In the first place, it is not the "first change" at all—that was the "leaden dawn," remember? Then, in the second place, the "Skull last place of all" (*F,* 55), site of this nascent story, is by virtue of the "first change of all" suddenly at best the next-to-last place. It is impossible to be precise about this first and last business—that would seem to be Beckett's point, or one of his points. Other actions follow; this final Fizzle is a real closer, action packed. Next there is "a light in the grey two white dwarfs" carrying a stretcher later identified as "the dung litter of laughable memory with shafts twice as long as the couch" (*F,* 58).

The cameo appearance by the dwarfs is followed by yet another event, the "last change of all in the end the expelled falls headlong down and lies back to sky full little stretch amidst his ruins" (*F,* 59). But again this is not the last change—two pages later "dark falls there again" (*F,* 61). The first change was not the first change; the last change was not the last change; the last place was not the last place. We have, however, ended yet again, admitting defeat: "Sepulchral skull is this then its last state all set for always litter and dwarfs ruins and little body grey cloudless sky glutted dust verge upon verge hell air not a breath" (*F,* 60). The apparent interrogative does not even merit a question mark, so obvious is the answer. "No for in the end for to end yet again by degrees or as though switched on dark falls there again" (*F,* 60–61).

Twenty years earlier, Beckett had attempted to describe his own practice by contrasting it with that of Joyce. "The more Joyce knew the more he could," he said. "He's tending toward omniscience and omnipotence as an artist. I'm working with impotence, ignorance."[39] Fizzle 8 provides a fine instance of such an art, not only in the obvious failures of its attempted last places and changes but also in the blatant awkwardnesses of syntax and idiom. How can dark be "switched on" (*F*, 61), for example, and is not one who falls "headlong" (*F*, 59) usually expected, for no good denotative reason, to land on his face? And a word like "pent" (*F*, 55) in the first sentence, like the "haught" (*SR*, 41) of *Ping* and the "blue celeste" (*SR*, 49, 51) of *Lessness*, among others, contributes to the pervasive air of contrived incompetence. It is Watt's "funambulistic stagger" (*W*, 31) again, the funny fiasco of the clown.

A final word about these stories: more even than the author's other, better known works, they are advertised as enormously forbidding, a body of arcana accessible only to adepts and requiring even of these repeated close analyses, a knowledge of statistics and access to a bank of computers. At times the critical voices rise to peroration in praise of this very quality, as if its production by Beckett and consumption by the critics were achieved as part of a demanding moral regimen. Thus one reads of "the courage required to spend a lifetime exploring such unpalatable truths," as if, for example, *The Lost Ones* could not have been written by a craven literary man familiar with Dante.[40]

All this is overstated, of course, the work of folks complimenting their own IQ and dedication. Certainly *Lessness* and *Ping* and the others require careful attention, but so do many other things, including many other things of wide appeal. Consider for example the following, another Irish song from the 1960s, this one from Belfast's Van Morrison, titled "Madame George," from the album *Astral Weeks*: "And the love that loves the love that loves the love that loves to love the love that loves the love to love the love that loves to love." Confronting this, the critic Lester Bangs, late but great, committed an intelligence: "Van Morrison is interested, *obsessed* with how much musical or verbal information he can compress into a small space, and, almost conversely, how far he can spread one note, word, sound, or picture. To capture one moment, be it a caress or twitch. He repeats certain phrases to extremes that from anybody else would seem ridiculous, because he's waiting for a vision to unfold."[41] This is criticism of a high order, and perhaps even helpful. But the point here is the popularity of the song itself. *Astral Weeks* was purchased and heard by thousands, not all or even most of them polymaths. Presumably they listened carefully, some of them, and that was enough. It is enough with Beckett too. And for those who continued to read, new and ampler rewards were in store. In 1980 *Company* appeared. Following upon *Fizzles* and the other truncations of the previous decade, it seemed a work of nearly epic scale.

Late Excellence

In 1980, after nearly 20 years of brevities, Beckett produced *Company*, a work of nearly 60 pages. It was written in English, and it surprised and delighted readers not only with its length but by its tone as well. Critics accustomed to the strained deadpan of the earlier works, the anthropological reporter of *The Lost Ones*, say, or the determined measurer of *Ping*, were quick to sense in the new work a quality of "miniaturized tenderness," a prose that was "lyrical, nostalgic, almost sentimental in spots."[42] *Company* was followed, in 1981 and 1983 respectively, by *Ill Seen Ill Said* and *Worstward Ho*, the former written in French the latter in English, and both of substantial length given the spare standard established by the works of the previous decade. *Ill Seen Ill Said* runs to just over 50 pages; *Worstward Ho* manages 40. The print, admittedly, is very large, but the ampler scale remains obvious. In his final works, then, after long restraint, Beckett achieved a breakthrough of sorts. Far from the vast white deserts of *Imagination Dead Imagine*, swept by storms, or the grey wastes of Fizzle 8 and *Lessness*, trudged by dwarfs and littered with ruins, these pieces introduce again a universe that includes Venus and an earth that includes Croker's Acres and Ballyogan Road, the former already known to readers from its mention in *Not I*, a play first acted in 1972. Old men wear greatcoats; reference is made to Dante, Michelangelo, and Christ, there are lambs and larches. We have done this tour before, perhaps. The ground is familiar, but the guide is more friendly.

Company

Company, especially, among these latest works, is a strikingly intimate work, arriving as a sort of backstage pass, an invitation to the studio, and thus offering unique pleasures. It is in places openly autobiographical and everywhere insistently retrospective, though critics have rightly insisted that autobiography is itself art and not raw confessional data. These personal touches, muted as always, amount to abashed celebration. Hamm, long before, alluded to *The Tempest*—"Our revels

70

now are ended" (*E*, 56)—to describe his situation. Here, much later, amid *Company*'s hints of conscious finale, Beckett in his own manner puts forward Prospero's affirmation: "Now does my project gather to a head. / My charms crack not, my spirits obey."[43]

The work opens on multiple perspectives immediately deployed. "A voice comes to one in the dark. Imagine."[44] A narrative is thus set in motion; two "characters" are moved to interaction, a first (voice) heard by a second (one). The terse imperative "Imagine" may be addressed to the reader or to yet another character, a third, shortly to be described as "another devising" (*C*, 8). Or to both. The story that is *Company*, then, signed as his own devising by the author, begins by initiating another story, the product of "another devising." A series is broached, and the process of fabulation is introduced as a theme. This in itself can occasion no surprise—characters in stories who are themselves storytellers abound in Beckett's works. Remember the *Texts for Nothing*, with its several stories within stories, Joe Breem or Breen in Text 1, for example, or Mother Calvet skimming garbage in Text 2, or the old tar Vincent in Text 3. Hamm, in *Endgame*, is also an author; he tells Clov with evident pride that he has "got on with my story" (*E*, 58).

What is new in *Company*, part of the guide's new intimacy, is the explicitness of motive and the tenacity with which the series of tellers is pursued to its source. What purposes impel the generation of these stories, after all, one after the other, when silence, ending, is so often the stated goal? The suggestion of a motive comes early on, in the second of the piece's 58 sections, in the same phrase that names the narrator: "another devising it all for company" (*C*, 8). The title itself, of course, here appearing in the text for the first of many times, adds emphasis to the phrase. It is for company that the devisers devise, imagine stories, create characters and move them, like Malone, "down the long familiar galleries, with my little suns and moons that I hang aloft" (*TN*, 236). It is for company that he puts himself to such exertion, much as Vladimir and Estragon elude their own sense of isolation with every distraction, every "little canter" (*G*, 42a) they can muster.

In telling his story, the deviser of *Company*—yet another "head abandoned to its ancient solitary resources" (*TN*, 361)—bases his (or her) narrative decisions on this criterion. Which alternative, alternative inspirations presenting themselves, will provide, being chosen, "the better company"? This is the decisive question. Given, for example, a problem of lighting, a choice between two shades of imperfect dark,

"The test is company. Which of the two darks is the better company" (*C*, 26–27).

This is the heart of the enterprise, then, the company itself, the fellow creature of our own devising who preserves us, however briefly, however imperfectly, from the horror of solitude. The passage from *Godot*, deservedly famous, in which Vladimir and Estragon discuss hanging themselves, centers precisely on this horror. A tortured dispute over precedence—each wishes the other to hang himself first—is resolved at last by Estragon, in the play's most sustained ratiocinative effort: "Gogo light—bough not break—Gogo dead. Didi heavy—bough break—Didi alone. Whereas—" (*G*, 12b).

"Didi alone"—that is the thing to avoid, so long as possible, so long as company can be devised. This is the true motive, the heart's deep cry, the need that moves madmen to sleep with dolls in asylums. Malone's explanation is succinct: "Yes, a little creature, I shall try and make a little creature, to hold in my arms, a little creature in my image, no matter what I say" (*TN*, 226). And if each effort ends in failure—if *Company* closes with "you as you always were" followed by the single word close "Alone" (*C*, 63), set off by itself like the "It is not" (*MPTK*, 22) of "Dante and the Lobster"—what matters in the interim is the urge to create, the need for "a little creature in my image" that links the whole series, devisers and deviseds.

What *Company* does, persistently, against the grain of a lifework's reticence—*Not I* is a resonant title for Beckett—is pursue this chain of narrated narrators to an origin, an unsaid, unsayable sayer, the nothing source of all. "And whose voice asking this?" opens the central passage, as searching as anything Beckett has written: "Who asks, Whose voice asking this? And answers, His soever who devises it all. In the same dark as his creature or in another. For company. Who asks in the end, Who asks? And in the end answers as above? And adds long after to himself, Unless another still. Nowhere to be found. Nowhere to be sought. The unthinkable last of all. Unnamable. Last person. I. Quick leave him" (*C*, 24).

We knew all the time, didn't we, that "in the end" it was "I," the author speaking in his own voice, Samuel Barclay Beckett himself, the ultimate homunculus, tiny within the others, and tinier still within the others within those others? First and last person, a voluble god. But wait—the whole drift of such musings calls into question such identifications and integrities. The "I" so long avoided and here at last revealed rises in this analytic light as no less "creature" and "figment" than any other finally unnamable character. Recall Vladimir: "At me too someone is looking, of me too someone is saying, He is sleeping, he knows nothing, let him sleep on" (*G*, 58b). Or recall *Proust*: "The aspirations of yesterday were valid for yesterday's ego, not for to-day's. We are disappointed at the nullity of what we are pleased to call attainment. But what is attainment? The identification of the subject and the object of his desire. The subject has died—and perhaps many times—on the way. For subject B to be disappointed by the banality of an object chosen by subject A is as illogical as to expect one's hunger to be dissipated by the spectacle of Uncle eating his dinner" (*P*, 3).

All this is logical enough, certainly, but finally insufficient. The world of these stories is dense with subjects who have died on their way, perhaps several times, but it did them no good. "Quick leave him" (*C*, 2, 24), says *Company*. But it is not so easy—he keeps coming back, from spiraling world tours, from beyond the grave. Trivialities may be rendered null by such expirations, but there are deeper things, more tenacious things, such as the memory of cries, the image of imploring eyes, the sound of Sunday bells on Croghan. Death? It is nothing to them. This is durable company, company for the long haul. Albert Camus returns to the Algiers of his youth to learn this lesson as a saving grace and writes about the experience in a lovely, lyric prose— "In the middle of winter I at last discovered that there was in me an invincible summer."[45] Beckett's creatures, devisers and deviseds, learn similar lessons, however different their reactions. In the middle of winter they discover, often to their pain, a blighted spring, unkillable. Nightmare, bad company, is company still.

But all is not nightmare. Far from it. Prominent among *Company*'s multiple retrospections is "the old lutanist" described as "now perhaps singing praises with some section of the blest at last" (*C*, 60). This is none other than the Belacqua (newly arrived in Purgatory when Dante passed through almost seven hundred years ago) who gave his name to the doomed philanderer, *Paradiso* fan, and spavined Gorgonzola eater of *More Pricks than Kicks*. That takes things back almost to the beginning, and with the addition of larches and greatcoats, allusions to Dante and Milton, *Company* reveals itself as a family reunion of sorts, a curtain call for what in *Molloy* is described as a "gallery of moribunds" (*TN*, 137). Here is final family reunion, perhaps, since the reference to Belacqua is followed by valediction: "To whom here in any case farewell" (*C*, 60). The more obviously autobiographical sections—the climb to "near the top of a great fir" (*C*, 21), for example, or the moment "at the tip of the high board" looking down to "the loved trusted face" of the father calling, "Be a brave boy" (*C,* 18) from the water below—serve at last to summon the author again, to link him to the chain of his own devising, to make him one with his company.

Beckett wrote, at last, no work warmer than *Company,* no work that is where the warmth always there burns closer to the surface. Even the brutal "Alone" at the volume's close—to a writer so alert to the way words undermine themselves it can come as no surprise that some will see even this one as mitigated internally, its overt assertion of solitude balanced by a covert suggestion of unity. That is the last thing in company, after all.

Ill Seen Ill Said

By its title alone, *Ill Seen Ill Said* would appear to pass two judgments, condemning first the quality of its vision and second the articulation of that vision. But the second, on aesthetic grounds, could be more apologia than apology, ill saying being defensible as ill seeing's most appropriate mode. What is ill seen, seen in glimpses subject to fades and blurrings, is a woman. She and her world are ill said in 61 single-paragraph sections that begin with a description of her home. She lives in a cabin with two windows, one facing east and the other west. Beneath the first is a bed or pallet, and by the second is a chair. She watches Venus from both: in the morning, as it is eclipsed by the sun, she "rails at the source of all life," but in the "evening when the skies are clear she savours its star's revenge."[46]

There is careful description of her surroundings, rendered in a mélange of voices ranging from dispassionate reporting to obvious parody. The cabin, for example, is surrounded by two "zones" (*IS,* 9), an inner zone of stones and an outer one of "meagre pastures." Of the cabin's position, one voice speaks straightforwardly: "At the inexistent centre of a formless place. Rather more circular than otherwise finally. Flat to be sure" (*IS,* 8). But this tone soon yields to another, to others: "Stones increasingly abound. Ever scanter even the rankest weed. Meagre pastures hem it round on which it slowly gains. With none to gainsay. To have gainsaid" (*IS,* 8). Inversions, archaisms, puns—this is ill saying indeed, and things will get worse. There is, for instance, at the outer edge of the pastures, a tombstone visited by the woman: "She is drawn to a certain spot. At times. There stands a stone. It it is draws her" (*IS,* 11).

Ill seeing and ill saying thus combine, as usual, to produce an aborted narrative, a collection of fragmentary starts and stops, visions and revisions. Readers may make guesses, may disagree, over, for example, whether the woman is dead or alive, or whether the mysterious figures referred to as "the twelve" allude to the apostles or the signs of the zodiac, but the author's self-proclaimed incompetence here as elsewhere has ensured the indeterminacy necessary to encourage finally unvalidated surmise.[47] The narrative itself is recurrently attentive to its flaws, but never more pointedly than in its fifteenth section, which addresses itself to the sources of a "confusion" already admitted: "Things and imaginings. As of always. Confusion amounting to nothing. Despite precautions. If only she could be pure figment. Unalloyed. This old so dying woman. So dead. In the madhouse of the skull and nowhere else" (*IS*, 20).

But she cannot be a figment. Neither pure thing nor pure imagining, she is a mix, memory alloyed by fable, like the others, seen by both eyes, the one "having no need of light to see" (*IS*, 8) and the other "this filthy eye of flesh" (*IS*, 30). Studies of Beckett's work, in their well-founded emphasis on the interior world, on the flight of his characters from the world of mud to the world of mind, have sometimes forgotten that the external world has in fact proved persistent in that work, despite its frequent denunciation. Moran, in *Molloy*, can even speak of being "patiently turned toward the outer world as towards the lesser evil" (*TN*, 114). It is only by appreciating this orientation that readers may comprehend the tenderness everywhere evident toward everything from larches to oil lamps, lambs to crocuses, Croghan to Croker's Acres. It is a false either/or, finally. Like the couple from *Enough* devoted both to climbing and to arithmetic, Beckett's characters find things to love, things they cannot not love, in the big world and the small. Even Murphy and his mentor Neary, for whom the macrocosm is a "big blooming buzzing confusion" (*M*, 4), cannot wholly free themselves from its attachments. For Murphy, despite his efforts, loves Celia: "The part of him that he hated craved for Celia, the part that he loved shriveled up at the thought of her" (*M*, 8). Neary is no better off, confessing so powerful a need for a Miss Dwyer that "all is dross, for the moment at any rate, that is not Miss Dwyer" (*M*, 5).

Ill Seen Ill Said, for its part, manages in its longest section to find even an "old deal spindlebacked kitchen chair" (*IS*, 7) moving—"more than the empty seat the barred back is piteous" (*IS*, 35). A greatcoat in use as a curtain is first described as "sprawling inside out,"

Part 1

but this is soon revised to "inside in for the pathos of the dangling arms" (*IS*, 47). The sight of "boots and stockings" (*IS*, 17) or "the flagstone before her door that dint by dint her little weight has grooved" (*IS*, 17–18) can bring on tears. Any "detail of the desert" will do, will summon tears to the "riveted" eye that broods on it: "Imagination at wit's end spreads its sad wings" (*IS*, 17).

In the twenty-seventh section the wish for "pure figment" (*IS*, 20) is reiterated: "Not possible any longer except as figment. Not endurable. Nothing for it but to close the eye for good and see her. Her and the rest. Close it for good and all and see her to death" (*IS*, 30). It is not endurable, but it must be endured. For the only "pure figment" available is the dream of purity—all else is mixed, eye of mind with eye of flesh, so that in the thirty-first section "without having to close the eye sees her afar" (*IS*, 34). And what is more, in a chain of devisers and deviseds reminiscent of *Company*, the character "she" also seems to possess both eyes, to be plagued by her own mélange of memory and fable. In the thirty-second section she "with closed eyes sees the tomb" (*IS*, 37) she visits so obsessively. Is the tomb her husband's? And does her left hand lack "its third finger" because she cut it off "one panic day" (*IS*, 32) just after his death in order to bury her wedding ring with him? And the eye that watches and waits on her so assiduously when "Any other would renounce" (*IS*, 17), could it belong to the shade of her husband, perhaps, just as the "you" of *Company* is accompanied at times by "your father's shade" (*IS*, 15)? Perhaps. At any rate, they form a company of sorts, she and this other: "But she has no own. Yes yes she has one. And who has her" (*IS*, 13).

But the comparisons with *Company* are misleading. *Ill Seen Ill Said* is a colder piece, harsher, finally a return to what may be Beckett's oldest, most obsessive issue: the matter of ending, there from the beginning, the oldest question, still unanswered. Being done with being—it is a paradoxical quest, of course, at least on the linguistic level, but these characters (and especially the narrators, the devising deviseds) have recurrently taken it for a worthy goal. Paradise Lost was the Eden of inexistence, lost at birth (or perhaps conception, the debate rages on), but perhaps available again, a second chance, for the deceased. Hamm, telling the story of the madman, locates it "way back," when Clov was not "in the land of the living" (*E*, 44). "God be with the days!" says Clov (*E*, 44). Maddy Rooney, in *All That Fall*, longs to be "in atoms" (*KLT*, 43). Ruby Tough and Belacqua bungle

76

the suicide plotted in an allegedly lucid interval. "TEMPORARILY SANE," says their note (*MPTK*, 97). Again and again Beckett's company gives voice to the standard Sophoclean pearl: "Not to be born surpasses thought and speech. / The second best is to have seen the light / And then go back quickly whence we came."[48]

But recurrent as it is, the view that extinction is best does not go unchallenged. Poised against Maddy Rooney's longing for decomposition is her husband's celebration of his office retreat, with its food and drink to hand, a situation so pleasant that not even "fully certified death" (*KLT*, 79) could offer more. In *Molloy*, Moran's meditation on the "great classical paralyses," which result in "just enough brain intact to allow you to exult," is in basic agreement. Given such a bliss, Moran says he would "dread death like a regeneration" (*TN*, 140).

Ill Seen Ill Said deals with these matters most pointedly in its final sections. On the last page, in a blizzard of ambiguities and paradoxes— "for to end yet again" (Fizzle 8's title recycled), "end begun," "first last moment"—the volume's final moment is finely subdivided. The "first last moment" is a prayer for a sufficiency of consciousness: "Grant only enough remain to devour all." This boon obtained, a perhaps ultimate "enough" might be within reach: "Lick chops and basta." But no, there is more, a request for "One moment more. One last." And this moment's use, given that it is granted? "Grace to breathe that void. Know happiness" (*IS*, 59). It is not enough, for this supplicant, simply to cease. Happiness, for this petitioner, is to experience cessation, to be present at absence. Or, as *Ill Seen Ill Said* puts it one page earlier, "Absence supreme good and yet" (*IS*, 58). The voice of wisdom counsels letting go, as it did in *Malone Dies*, in one of Beckett's loveliest, least guarded moments:

> But I am not wise. For the wise thing now would be to let go, at this instant of happiness. And what do I do? I go back again to the light, to the fields I so longed to love, to the sky all astir with little white clouds as white and light as snowflakes, to the life I could never manage, through my own fault perhaps, through pride, or pettiness, but I don't think so. The beasts are at pasture, the sun warms the rocks and makes them glitter. Yes, I leave my happiness and go back to race of men too, they come and go, often with burdens. . . . Here I go none the less, mistakenly. Night, storm and sorrow, and the catalepsies of the soul, this time I shall see that they are good. (*TN*, 199)

The voice of wisdom, in *Ill Seen Ill Said*, continues unheeded, the unqualified assertion of "supreme good" undermined by the simple "and yet" that may be nothing more than an admission of cowardice but is more likely a more oblique confession of attachment to things of "the light," the doomed and haunted things of the light. Here, too, in its muted syntax, is the urge to go back, to "devour all," that is, to swallow everything whole. A truly omnivorous appetite here could insist that "all" must mean the whole of life, for how could the "first last moment" be anything later than birth? It should be clear that the "end begun" occurs at the beginning. Like Dante's Belacqua, who did not seem to mind delaying his purgation and ascent, Beckett's creatures are always tempted to go back, to be again. "Farewell to farewell," says the piece's final section. That is oxymoronic, yet again. We grasp such notions imperfectly and articulate them imprecisely. Thus "Know happiness" (*IS*, 59) invites its negative homonym; negation and assertion cast their doubts endlessly, each upon the other; and our master of incapacities fails on, his ill saying matching his ill seeing with great dour panache.

Worstward Ho

Notice the panache, for instance, in the next work's title, its latter word rendered dour by the withholding of the expected exclamation, while the first term indicates direction, progress, ill seeing and ill saying grown iller, that's ill saying for you, taking a turn for the worse. And this, of course, is better. Nowhere is the project outlined more explicitly than in *Worstward Ho*—"Try again. Fail again. Fail better."[49] This is a more modest articulation of that by now ancient goal, put forward with characteristic overstatement by Hamm, "play and lose and have done with losing" (*E*, 82). Of course, it is not that simple, that much is clear by now. Losing, mere losing, failing, mere failing, are insufficient, far, far from sufficient. Losing is far from lost, failing far from failed; even a grammarian can see it. Playing, it seems to follow, continues indefinitely toward a loss as elusive as it is inevitable. "Fail worse again," says *Worstward Ho*. "Still worse again" (*WH*, 8).

A voice begins by telling itself to continue. "On," it says, "Say on" (*WH*, 7). A story of sorts is soon broached, three stories in fact, the voice speaking to itself first of a body, soon provided with bones and sufficient "remains of mind" (*WH*, 9) to allow for pain, then of a "Head sunk on crippled hands" identified as the "Germ of all" (*WH*, 10), and finally of a pair, "an old man and a child" who walk together "Joined by held holding hands" (*WH*, 13). Of place only a "Dim light source unknown" (*WH*, 10–11) is specified, along with the assurance of infallible security: "Unknow better now. Know only no out of" (*WH*, 11).

This cast, in this place, is set to motion, hesitantly, each element "worsened" in turn, several times, the voice returning "To try worsen" (*WH*, 23) as a means, desperate means, of getting on. "Back is on," it says, "Somehow on" (*WH*, 37). Thus the body first stands (on page 8), then kneels (on page 15), later bows down (on page 22), still later is provided with gender, female (on page 35), and finally (on page 47) suddenly recedes almost from view. The head, for its part, first loses its hands and face, is reduced to "Skull and stare alone" (*WH*, 24) without losing its suggested primacy as the source of everything: "Germ of all. All? If of all of it too. Where if not there it too? There in the sunken head the sunken head" (*WH*, 19). Even stripped of hands and face, it continues as the "Scene and seer of all" (*WH*, 24). Then, improbably for a skull, the eyes "Unclench" (*WH*, 27), revealing after several subsequent worsenings "Dim black holes" (*WH*, 27–28), which are themselves soon reduced to "One dim black hole mid-foreskull" (*WH*, 44). Still later this hole, like the now feminine bowed kneeling body, also recedes in an instant—"No move and sudden all far" (*WH*, 47).

The third "character(s)," the old man and child, first lose their shoes, then "plod apart" (*WH*, 34), soon to be separated by a vast "rift" (*WH*, 41), and later disappear from "napes up" and "pelves down" so as to be, improbably again, "Legless plodding on" (*WH*, 43). Finally, like the others, they recede, nearly disappear. The body, the child, and the old man, all worsened since first seen, worsened several times by the voice's "worsening words" (*WH*, 28), are finally "Three pins" (*WH*, 47), while the head, itself worsened to "black hole mid-foreskull" (*WH*, 44), is "one pinhole." The voice, the materials for worsening nearly gone, for going on by worsening nearly gone, concludes in impotence: "Nohow on " (*WH*, 47).

Sure. The concert is over, right? The author has left the building? No chance. The fans know the genre by now. We are on our feet, still clapping. We remember "Dante and the Lobster," with its false floor ending, the big white space below, and then the voice of God finale. Beckett was a generous, persevering maestro, an obstinate master of unknowing. Here, 50 years after *More Pricks than Kicks*, he is still at work, still returning for another encore. What a trooper he is, this most reticent of stars! Look down the white space. There it is, the latest last line, all for now, all for *Worstward Ho*: "Said nohow on" (*WH*, 47).

But "nohow" is "know-how," somehow. And this latest, most worsened work, where does it end? With a kneeling woman, a child and an old man holding hands. Woman, child, man—the nuclear family, basic unit ancient even to Zinjanthropus. Remember: "another image yet another a boy sitting on a bed in the dark or a small old man I can't see with his head be it young or be it old his head in his hands I appropriate that heart."[50] Be it young or be it old, be it man or be it woman, Beckett indeed appropriated that heart, mounted long vigil over its hopeless loves, ordered quiet celebration of its fragile joys, respected its griefs in grieving prose, persisted in his chronicle of its endurance. Like his own man Watt, he refused to "abate one jot" of his chosen tale of "the dim mind wayfaring," the "flame with dark winds/hedged about" (*W*, 249, 246, 250). For the author bent patiently to such a task, the short story, its generic boundaries generously conceived, proved a singularly fruitful form.

No essay devoted to such an artist of endless endgame, of prolonged attenuation, should end too easily. But there is a way. A last piece has recently been released. *Stirrings Still*. Sound familiar? The persistence. The oxymoron. Open to the first sentence: "One night as he sat at his table head on hands he saw himself rise and go."[51] Sound familiar? The divided, self-conscious self. The departure. *Stirrings Still* presents for a final time a character awaiting the "one true end to time and grief" (*SS*, 25) with mixed emotions. In the piece's three sections, each one shorter than its predecessor, "he" first observes his own departure from the "indoors" (*SS*, 31) to "the outer world" (*SS*, 27), second finds himself in a "field of grass" (*SS*, 31) doubly unfamiliar because no boundary is visible and because the grass is not "the short green grass he seemed to remember . . . but long and light grey in colour verging here and there on white" (*SS*, 33), and third hears "from deep within" (*SS*, 39) a brief, ambiguous message. The action, then, can be summarized even more succinctly: he goes out, then he goes "deep within." His efforts to understand the message's import, or even its exact words—"oh how and here a word he could not catch it were to end where never till then" (*SS*, 39) is the text as received—produce at last only a "hubbub in his mind" (*SS*, 43). The piece closes with "nothing left from deep within but only ever fainter oh to end. No matter how no matter where. Time and grief and self so-called. Oh all to end" (*SS*, 43).

And *Stirrings Still* does end, right there, with ending and yearning for ending united, like an answered prayer. Again, for a final time, we are both stirred and stilled, offered something of tragedy's high hoopla in a chastened comedy. Pity, fear, perhaps a smiling catharsis, the austere, gentle *risolino* loved of old. And that is best, surely, amid inevitable worsenings to have this kind of company, subdued and enduring.

Notes to Part 1

1. "Assumption," *transition* 16–17 (1929): 268; hereafter cited in the text.

2. "The Calmative," in *Stories and Texts for Nothing* (New York: Grove Press, 1967), 29; hereafter cited in the text as *STN*.

3. *More Pricks than Kicks* (New York: Grove Press, 1972), 9; hereafter cited in the text as *MPTK*.

4. *Waiting for Godot* (New York: Grove Press, 1954), 34b; hereafter cited in the text as *G*.

5. James Joyce, *Dubliners* (New York: Penguin, 1976), 223.

6. The poem is "Che Sciagura," a juvenile effort first published in *T.C.D.*, a Trinity College weekly, in 1929. Malone, in the French original of *Malone Dies*, says *"quel malheur"* [what a misfortune] when he loses his stick. The phrase closes the eleventh chapter of *Candide*, spoken by the Eunuch before the naked Cunegonde. *"O che sciagura,"* he says, *"d'essere senza coglioni!"* (What a shame to have no balls!).

7. Deirdre Bair, *Samuel Beckett* (New York: Harcourt, Brace, Jovanovich, 1978), 146.

8. "An Imaginative Work!" review of *The Amaranthers* by Jack B. Yeats, *Dublin Magazine* 11 (1936): 80.

9. *Watt* (New York: Grove Press, 1959), 48; hereafter cited in the text as *W*.

10. "A Case in a Thousand," *The Bookman* 86 (1934): 241; hereafter cited in the text.

11. See, for example, Bair, *Samuel Beckett*, where an especially fuzzy sentence opens with the character Dr. Nye in the subject chair but substitutes the author Beckett at an indeterminate middle point to close in psychological rather than literary analysis: "Dr. Nye's fascination with Mrs. Bray as a mother-sweetheart, his longing for his childhood and the curious womblike evocation of the bizarre incident of the bed all seem to be clumsy attempts to integrate his real-life attitudes towards his mother with his fiction" (185).

12. *Murphy* (New York: Grove Press, 1957), 178; hereafter cited in the text as *M*.

13. *Molloy*, in *Three Novels by Samuel Beckett* (New York: Grove Press, 1965), 140; hereafter cited in the text as *TN*.

14. *Endgame* (New York: Grove Press, 1958), 1; hereafter cited in the text as *E*.

15. "First Love," in *First Love and Other Shorts* (New York: Grove Press, 1974), 22; hereafter cited in the text as *FL*.

16. *Proust* (New York: Grove Press, 1957), 32; hereafter cited in the text as *P*.

17. Samuel Beckett and Georges Duthuit, "Three Dialogues," *transition forty-nine* (1949): 103.

18. *Mercier and Camier* (New York: Grove Press, 1974), 32; hereafter cited in the text as *MC*.

19. *Embers*, in *Krapp's Last Tape and Other Dramatic Pieces* (New York: Grove Press, 1960), 121; hereafter cited in the text as *KLT*.

20. *From an Abandoned Work*, in *Six Residua* (London: John Calder, 1978), 11; hereafter cited in the text as *SR*.

21. Colin Duckworth, "Beckett's New *Godot*," in *Beckett's Later Fiction and Drama*, ed. James Acheson and Kateryna Arthur (New York: St. Martin's, 1987), 191, 190.

22. This information is credited to Christina Rosset of Grove Press, in Rubin Rabinovitz, "The Self Contained: Beckett's Fiction in the 1960s," in Acheson and Arthur, *Beckett's Later Fiction and Drama*, 60.

23. See, for example, the discussion of *Still*, "Sounds," and "Still 3" in Brian Finney, "*Still* to *Worstward Ho*: Beckett's Prose Fiction Since *The Lost Ones*," in Acheson and Arthur, *Beckett's Later Fiction and Drama*, where Beckett's revisions are characterized as tending to "condensation and refinement" (67).

24. *All Strange Away*, in *Rockaby and Other Short Pieces* (New York: Grove Press, 1981), 39; hereafter cited in the text as *R*.

25. James Knowlson and John Pilling, *Frescoes of the Skull: The Later Prose and Drama of Samuel Beckett* (New York: Grove Press, 1980), 145; subsequent references in text.

26. Dr. Franz Blaha, "Dachau: The Medical Experiments, 1941–45," in *Eye-witness to History*, ed. John Carey (Cambridge: Harvard University Press, 1987), 557.

27. J. Z. Holwell, "The Black Hole of Calcutta, 21 June 1756," in Carey, *Eye-witness to History*, 225.

28. Linda Ben-Zvi, *Samuel Beckett* (Boston: Twayne, 1986), 121. For other discussions of the story as "an anachronism in Beckett's fiction," see Susan D. Brienza, *Samuel Beckett's New Worlds* (Norman: University of Oklahoma Press, 1987), 71; and Rabinovitz, "The Self Contained," 50.

29. The association of *Enough* with Belacqua is discussed persuasively by Susan Brienza. See *Samuel Beckett's New Worlds*, 73.

30. *Happy Days* (New York: Grove Press, 1961), 16.

31. *The Lost Ones* (New York: Grove Press, 1972), 7; hereafter cited in the text as *LO*.

32. Raymond Federman and John Fletcher, *Samuel Beckett: His Works and His Critics* (Berkeley: University of California Press, 1970), 325.

33. For a discussion of "meaning," among other terms, see John Mood, "'Silence Within': A Study of the *Residua* of Samuel Beckett," *Studies in Short Fiction* 7 (1970): 398; for "perhaps," among other terms, see Brienza, *Samuel Beckett's New Worlds*, 174; for terms used but once see David Lodge, "Some *Ping* Understood," *Encounter* 30 (1968): 85–89.

34. Brienza, *Samuel Beckett's New Worlds*, 179. For an especially determined quantitative analysis of *Lessness*, see J. M. Coetzee, "Samuel Beckett's *Lessness*: An Exercise in Decomposition," *Computers and the Humanities* 7 (1973): 195–98.

35. Samuel Beckett to Alan Schneider, 29 December 1957. In *The Village Voice Reader* (Garden City, N.Y.: Doubleday, 1962), 168.

36. Rabinovitz ("The Self Contained," 60) cites Christina Rosset of Grove Press for this claim.

37. *Fizzles* (New York: Grove Press, 1976), 7; hereafter cited in the text as *F*.

38. Hugh Kenner, *A Reader's Guide to Samuel Beckett* (New York: Farrar, Straus and Giroux, 1973), 82,81.

39. Israel Shenker, "Moody Man of Letters," *New York Times*, May 6, 1956, sec. 2, 1, 3.

40. Brian Finney, *Since, 'How It is': A Study of Samuel Beckett's Later Fiction* (London: Covent Garden Press, 1972), 41.

41. Lester Bangs, "*Astral Weeks*," in *Psychotic Reactions and Carburetor Dung*, ed. Greil Marcus (New York: Random House, 1988), 22. Bangs also quotes from "Madam George," but his hearing of the song differs slightly from my own.

42. Enoch Brater, "The *Company* Beckett Keeps: The Shape of Memory and One Fabulist's Decay of Lying," in *Samuel Beckett: Humanistic Perspectives* ed. Morris Beja, S. E. Gontarski, and Pierre Astier (Columbus: Ohio State University Press, 1983), 170. Also Brienza, *Samuel Beckett's New Worlds*, 217

43. William Shakespeare, *The Tempest* 5.1.11.1–2.

44. *Company* (New York: Grove Press, 1980), 7; hereafter cited in the text as *C*.

45. Albert Camus, "Return to Tipasa," in *The Myth of Sisyphus and Other Essays* (New York: Random House, 1955), 144.

46. *Ill Seen Ill Said* (New York: Grove Press, 1981), 7; hereafter cited in the text as *IS*.

47. Nicholas Zurbrugg, for example, opts for a dead woman, while noting that two other readers have taken a pro-life stance. See "*Ill Seen Ill Said* and the Sense of an Ending," in Acheson and Arthur, *Beckett's Later Fiction and Drama*, 145–46, 157–58. Marjorie Perloff suggests that "the twelve" refer primarily to the zodiac, though she wisely notes that they are "purposely unspecified." See "Between Verse and Prose: Beckett and the New Poetry," in *On Beckett: Essays and Criticism*, ed. S. E. Gontarski (New York: Grove Press, 1986), 206.

48. Sophocles, *Oedipus at Colonus*, trans. Robert Fitzgerald, in *Greek Tragedies*, Vol. 3, ed. David Grene and Richmond Lattimore (Chicago: University of Chicago Press, 1960), 166.

49. *Worstward Ho* (New York: Grove Press, 1983), 7; hereafter cited in the text as *WH*.

50. *How It Is* (New York: Grove Press, 1964), 18.

51. *Stirrings Still* (New York: Blue Moon Books, 1991), 9; hereafter cited in the text as *SS*.

Part 2

THE WRITER

Introduction

A man who describes art as "the apotheosis of solitude" is an unlikely candidate for literary lion, and it is fair to say that Samuel Beckett shunned public attention with considerable tenacity and ingenuity. When his Nobel Prize was announced in 1969, he journeyed not to Stockholm but to Tunisia. Not that it did him any good. Photographs appeared soon enough, revealing the fugitive celebrity cornered in a hotel in the town of Nabeul, peering with myopic dismay into the blazing cameras.

Interviews with Beckett are both rare and disappointing, sharing as they do a decided sense of the interviewee's discomfort, the clear suggestion that his formidable courtesy is for the moment holding his equally strong reluctance at bay. Excerpts from several of these interviews are included here; statements made under duress may yet make compelling reading, just as a man speaking against his will may yet speak his mind.

The author's admirers, and they are legion, have been quite another matter, of course. They have generally been downright fulsome, as if in compensation for their hero's silence. That brevity on their part might be an appropriate response to his taciturnity has occurred to nearly none. The best among these, that is to say the least fulsome, those that are most alert to their subject's reticence, are also excerpted here, and in one instance printed complete. These should offer at least some portrait of the artist at his work, and at most a glimpse of that artist as he is respected and admired as a man. The world, too, which he witnessed and in which he labored, may be glimpsed in the frozen, bombed-out church at St. Lô and in the deserted streets of Paris shared with Giacometti.

Also included, at the beginning, with no excuse beyond this editor's admiration, are a number of the author's own comments on the work of other authors, on his own, and on literary art in general. That Beckett repudiated some of these efforts as "bilge" and opposed the publication of others, has availed him nothing here. Even *Molloy* is quoted at one point as if it were a manifesto instead of a novel. These snippets are arranged chronologically, no other logic being available, in the hope that they might thus exhibit, like the fiction, the patient reduction of ornament, of lyric soar, of positive statement. The aggressive insistence on the artist's methods and prerogatives, prominent in the 1929 "Dante . . . Bruno . Vico . . Joyce" or the 1931 *Proust*, for example, and still evident even in the 1938 review, has by the 1957 letter to Alan Schneider and the 1961–62 conversations with Lawrence Harvey given way to a focus on the artist's inabilities, an aesthetic of dogged persistence in the face of immortal obstacles.

In His Own Words

1929

Here is direct expression—pages and pages of it. And if you don't understand it, Ladies and Gentlemen, it is because you are too decadent to receive it. You are not satisfied unless form is so strictly divorced from content that you can comprehend the one almost without bothering to read the other. The rapid skimming and absorption of the scant cream of sense is made possible by what I may call a continuous process of copious intellectual salivation. The form that is an arbitrary and independent phenomenon can fulfil no higher function than that of stimulus for a tertiary or quartary conditioned reflex of dribbling comprehension. . . .

Mr Joyce has desophisticated language. And it is worth while remarking that no language is so sophisticated as English. It is abstracted to death. Take the word "doubt": it gives us hardly any sensuous suggestion of hesitancy, of the necessity for choice, of static irresolution. Whereas the German "Zweifel" does, and, in lesser degree, the Italian "dubitare." Mr Joyce recognizes how inadequate 'doubt' is to express a state of extreme uncertainty, and replaces it by "in twosome twiminds." Nor is he by any means the first to recognize the importance of treating words as something more than mere polite symbols. Shakespeare uses fat, greasy words to express corruption: "Duller shouldst thou be than the fat weed that rots itself in death on Lethe wharf." We hear the ooze squelching all through Dickens's description of the Thames in *Great Expectations*. This writing that you find so obscure is a quintessential extraction of language and painting and gesture, with all the inevitable clarity of the old inarticulation. Here is the savage economy of hieroglyphics.

From "Dante . . . Bruno . Vico . . Joyce," first published in 1929 in *transition* and as the first chapter of *Our Exagmination Round His Factification for Incamination of Work in Progress* (Paris: Shakespeare and Company, 1929). Reprinted in *Disjecta*, ed. Ruby Cohn (New York: Grove Press, 1984), 26–28. Reprinted by permission of Grove Press.

1931

The artistic tendency is not expansive, but a contraction. And art is the apotheosis of solitude. There is no communication because there are no vehicles of communication.

The only fertile research is excavatory, immersive, a contraction of the spirit, a descent. The artist is active, but negatively, shrinking from the nullity of extracircumferential phenomena, drawn in to the core of the eddy.

Tragedy is not concerned with human justice. Tragedy is the statement of an expiation, but not the miserable expiation of a codified breach of a local arrangement, organised by the knaves for the fools. The tragic figure represents the expiation of original sin, of the original and eternal sin of him and all his "soci malorum," the sin of having been born.

1937

It is becoming more difficult, even senseless, for me to write a standard English. More and more my own language appears to me as a veil, to be torn apart to approach the things (or Nothingness) behind it. Grammar and style! They seem to me as superannuated as a Victorian bathing suit or the dignity of a gentleman. A mask. A time, let's hope, is coming, is in certain circles already here, God be thanked, when language will be best used when best abused. Since we can't eliminate it all at once, let's at least not neglect anything that might contribute to its corruption. To bore hole after hole in it, until what cowers behind it begins to seep through—I can imagine no higher goal for a contemporary writer.

Or must literature alone be forever left behind on worn out paths abandoned long ago by music and painting? Is there some paralyzing sanctity in the artificiality of words that doesn't belong to the elements

From *Proust*, first published in 1931 (London: Chatto & Windus). Reprinted in 1957 (New York: Grove Press), 47, 48, 49. Reprinted by permission of Grove Press.

From a letter to Axel Kaun, written in German. Translated from the German by Robert Cochran with the help of Christoph Irmscher. Previously printed (in German and in English translation by Martin Esslin) in *Disjecta*, ed. Ruby Cohn (New York: Grove Press, 1984), 52–53, 53–54. A typescript of the letter is in the Baker Memorial Library at Dartmouth College. Kaun was a friend Beckett met during his travels in Germany in 1936. Reprinted by permission of Grove Press.

of the other arts? Is there any reason at all why that terrible arbitrary materiality of the word's surface can't be eroded, like for instance the great black pauses eaten in the tonal surface of Beethoven's seventh symphony, so that for whole pages we can see nothing but a path of sound threading dizzying abysses of silence. . . .

On the way toward my much desired wordless literature, some form of Nominalist irony might of course be a necessary stage. But it's not enough when the game gives up some of its high solemnity. It must end. Let's do like that crazy (?) mathematician who employed a new principle of measurement for each separate step in his calculations. An attack upon words for beauty's sake.

Meanwhile I do nothing. But from time to time now I have the solace of unwittingly offending a foreign language as I would happily offend my own knowingly and deliberately—and shall, Deo juvante.

1938

The time is perhaps not altogether too green for the vile suggestion that art has nothing to do with clarity, does not dabble in the clear and does not make clear, any more than the light of day (or night) makes the subsolar, -lunar and -stellar excrement. Art is the sun, moon and stars of the mind, the whole mind. And the monacodologists who think of it in terms of enlightenment are what Nashe, surprised by a cordial humour, called the Harveys, "the sarpego and sciatica of the Seven Liberall Sciences."

1947

For what I was doing I was doing neither for Molloy, who mattered nothing to me, nor for myself, of whom I despaired, but on behalf of a cause which, while having need of us to be accomplished, was in its essence anonymous, and would subsist, haunting the minds of men, when its miserable artisans should be no more. It will not be said, I think, that I did not take my work to heart. But rather, tenderly, Ah those old craftsmen, their race is extinct and the mould broken.

From a review of *Intercessions*, by Denis Devlin. First published in *transition* (1938). Reprinted in *Disjecta*, ed. Ruby Cohn (New York: Grove Press, 1984), 94. Reprinted by permission of Grove Press.

From *Three Novels* (New York: Grove Press, 1965), 114–15. Reprinted by permission of Grove Press.

1957

It would be impertinent of me to advise you about the article you are
doing and I don't intend to. But when it comes to journalists I feel the
only line is to refuse to be involved in exegesis of any kind. And to
insist on the extreme simplicity of dramatic situation and issue. If that's
not enough for them, and it obviously isn't, it's plenty for us, and we
have no elucidations to offer of mysteries that are all of their making.
My work is a matter of fundamental sounds (no joke intended) made
as fully as possible, and I accept responsibility for nothing else. If people want to have headaches among the overtones, let them. And provide their own aspirin. Hamm as stated, and Clov as stated, together
as stated, nec tecum nec sine te, in such a place, and in such a world,
that's all I can manage, more than I could.

1961–1962

During conversations in 1961 and 1962 Beckett frequently expressed
himself on his activity as a writer and its relation to his existence as a
human being. In the following pages I transcribe some of his remarks
as they were recorded in notes taken during these conversations. . . .

An image Beckett used repeatedly to express his sense of the un-
reality of life on the surface was "existence by proxy." Very often one
is unable to take a single step without feeling that someone else is
taking the step. Going through the motions, "being absent," are common experiences. . . .

Along with this sense of existence by proxy goes "an unconquerable
intuition that being is so unlike what one is standing up," an intuition
of "a presence, embryonic, undeveloped, of a self that might have
been but never got born, an *être manqué.*"

Beckett spoke also of the attempt to find this lost self in images of
getting down, getting below the surface, concentrating, listening, getting your ear down so you can hear the infinitesimal murmur. There is

From a letter to Alan Schneider, part of an exchange dealing mostly with the American
production of *Endgame*, directed by Schneider. First published in *Village Voice* (1958).
Reprinted in *Disjecta*, ed. Ruby Cohn (New York: Grove Press, 1984), 108–9. Reprinted by permission of Grove Press.

From Lawrence E. Harvey, *Samuel Beckett: Poet and Critic* (Princeton: Princeton University Press, 1970), 247–50, 435. Reprinted by permission of Princeton University
Press.

a gray struggle, a groping in the dark for a shadow. On another occasion he said the encounter was like meeting oneself, like approaching home. And then one comes face to face with one's stupidities, one's obscenities, and one becomes convinced of the authentic weakness of being. . . .

Even when Beckett succeeds in getting beneath the surface, a prerequisite to writing, the problem is far from solved. With both object and subject, nature and agent, called into question, materials are lacking. "What complicates it all is the need to make. Like a child in mud but no mud. And no child. Only need." . . .

If one remains at this deep level of the need to make, one can't perceive objects, one is shut away from the world. In this realm "the writer is like a foetus trying to do gymnastics." This collision between a need to make and a lack of materials accounts for a characteristic quality in the writing of Beckett's maturity.

The problem of the absence of materials extends to language and form, both of which are associated with the macrocosm. "Joyce believed in words. All you had to do was rearrange them and they would express what you wanted." Beckett, however, has less confidence in language. "If you really get down to the disaster, the slightest eloquence becomes unbearable. Whatever is said is so far from experience." Beckett's dilemma is almost the dilemma of expressing the inexpressible. The need to express is as real as the obstacles to expression. On one occasion Beckett said, "I write because I have to," and added, "What do you do when 'I can't' meets 'I must'?" He admitted to using words where words are illegitimate. "At that level you break up words to diminish shame. Painting and music have so much better a chance."

On the other hand, he vigorously denied that his enterprise had anything at all to do with surrealist formlessness. At this deeper level "there is a form, but it doesn't move, stand upright, have hands. Yet it must have its form. Being *has* a form. Someone will find it someday. Perhaps I won't, but someone will. It is a form that has been abandoned, left behind, a proxy in its place." While the situation of a writer caught in such a dilemma is a distressing one, it also has about it the excitement of exploration and discovery. "Being," according to Beckett, has been excluded from writing in the past. The attempt to expand the sphere of literature to include it, which means eliminating the artificial forms and techniques that hide and violate it, is the adventure of modern art. Someday someone will find an adequate form, a "syntax of weakness." Beckett has too anguished a sense of the tremendous gulf between words and reality, art and being, too keen an awareness of the temptations and risks of language to underestimate the difficulty of the undertaking or overestimate what has so far been achieved. ("I can't let my left hand know what my right hand is doing. There is a danger of rising up into rhetoric. Speak it even and pride comes. Words are a form of complacency.") . . .

Referring to the snowman that the child builds, he remarked, "Well, this is like trying to build a dustman." His predicament he described as that of "one on his knees, head against a wall—more like a cliff—with someone saying 'go on.'" Later he said, "Well, the wall will have to move a little, that's all."

As Others Say Him

Richard W. Seaver

In the mid-fifties, when I was working with Beckett over a translation—from French to English—of his story "La Fin," I noted his increasing despair not only at our seeming inability to transpose the story from one language to another but at what seemed to Beckett to be the painful inadequacy of the original. Beckett had once told me how hard it was for him to translate his own work and how much time it took him. In my youthful exuberance—and ignorance—I suggested that, if it would give him more time to devote to creative work, I would attempt to translate something, essentially to save him time.

For weeks I labored over the text, which when I had read it in the French had struck me as beautifully simple. But the more I worked the more I realized how deceptive that initial impression had been. When I had finally completed the translation I informed Beckett, who suggested that we meet to go over it. We met at Le Dôme at Montparnasse, ensconced ourselves at an isolated table near the back, and began to work. Or rather: Beckett began to read. After a few minutes of perusing first my translation, then the original, his wire-framed glasses pushed up into the thick shock of hair above—the better to see, no doubt—he shook his head. My heart sank. Clearly, the translation was inadequate. "You can't translate that," he said, fingering the original with utter disdain. "It makes no sense." Again he squinted at the two texts. Several more minutes of ruminations and cross-checking produced a more optimistic report. "That's good," he murmured. "Those first three sentences read very nicely indeed." The opening passage to which he referred went, in my translation: "They dressed me and gave me money. I knew what the money was to be used for, it was for my travelling expenses. When it was gone, they said, I would have to get some more, if I wanted to go on travelling."

From Richard W. Seaver, "Beckett and 'Merlin,'" in *On Beckett: Essays and Criticism,* ed. S. E. Gontarski (New York: Grove Press, 1986), 25–27. Reprinted by permission of Grove Press.

"What do you think of the word *clothed*," Beckett said, "instead of *dressed*? 'They *clothed* me and gave me money.' Do you like the ring of it better?"

Yes, clearly: *clothed* was the better word.

"In the next sentence," he said, "you're literally right. In French I spelled it out, said 'traveling expenses' all right. But maybe we can make it a bit tighter here, just say something like, 'It was to get me going' or 'It was to get me started.' Do you like either of them at all?"

On we went, phrase by phrase, Beckett praising my translation as prelude to shaping it to what he really wanted, reworking here a word, there a whole sentence, chipping away, tightening, shortening, always finding the better word if one existed, exchanging the ordinary for the poetic, until the work sang. Never, I am sure, to his satisfaction, but certainly to my ear. Under Beckett's tireless wand that opening passage soon became: "They clothed me and gave me money. I knew what the money was for, it was to get me started. When it was gone I would have to get more, if I wanted to go on" [*STN*, 47].

During those long but edifying sessions, there were low moments and high, but for Beckett, faced with going back over a text he had left behind some years before, from which he had progressed to other levels and other considerations, it was too often painful. Finally, in response to one particularly long moment of despair, I blurted, "But Mr. Beckett! You're crazy! Don't you realize who you are? Why . . . you're a thousand times more important than . . . than Albert Camus, for example!" Searching for superlatives, I had grasped at this French writer who, at least at the time, was world famous. Camus had not yet won the Nobel Prize, but he was clearly headed for it, and readers and critics alike clamored for each new work, a response in total contrast to the virtual silence that greeted, and had always greeted, each new Beckett publication.

At that youthfully enthusiastic but obviously outlandish declaration, Beckett gazed compassionately across the table, his gaunt, hawklike features mirroring a response midway between disbelief and pity. "You don't know what you're saying, Dick." He shook his head sadly. "No one's interested in this . . . this rubbish." And he gestured contemptuously toward the untidy pile of manuscript pages on the table beside him.

Alberto Giacometti

Giacometti and Beckett met casually at the Café de Flore. They could hardly have been better made to appreciate and respect each other, and it seems inevitable that they should have become friends. It was a friendship very gradual in growth, for neither man was looking for solace or reassurance. On the contrary, what they eventually found in each other's company was an affirmation of the supreme value of a hopeless undertaking. They met most often by chance, usually at night, and went for long walks, the only destination of which was the conclusion that, having, as it were, nowhere to go, they were compelled to go there. It was a very private, almost secretive, and secret friendship. However, it did not exist in the vacuum of austere speculation. It came to be recognized by others as a confirmation of something which—even if they did not understand it—they could recognize as valuable. Many years later, when both men had become famous, a prostitute who knew them both saw them seated together on the terrace of a café. Going inside, she said to the proprietor: "It's your luck to have two of the great men of our time sitting together right now on your terrace, and I thought you ought to know it." . . .

The decor of *Waiting for Godot* is stark. It consists, in fact, of a single tree. By inviting Alberto to make this tree, Beckett hoped to include his friend in the goings-on of the hoboes. Alberto so resembled them, to tell the truth, as did Beckett, that while wandering occasionally through deserted streets at 3 a.m. they might well have expected to chance upon Godot. The author wrote early in March to the sculptor to make his request, adding hopefully: "It would give us all enormous pleasure." And by "all" he may be assumed to have meant not only himself and the play's producers and performers but also the characters, for whom Giacometti's tree would symbolize both life and death: because the bough from which a man can hang himself also bears leaves emblematic of rebirth.

Beckett's choice was inspired. Though Giacometti had never worked for the theater, he agreed at once. The production would be a fitting consecration of the friendship between author and sculptor.

With [his brother] Diego's assistance, of course, Alberto made a mar-

From James Lord, *Giacometti* (New York: Farrar, Straus & Giroux, 1985), 190, 428 29. Reprinted by permission of Farrar, Straus & Giroux.

velously curvaceous, dendriform creation in plaster. Then he and Beckett, both of them eternally unsatisfied, fiddled and fiddled with it. "All one night," Alberto said, "we tried to make that plaster tree larger or smaller, its branches more slender. It never seemed right, and each of us said to the other: maybe." Being man-made, to be sure, it never would seem right. Beckett and Alberto were made to order to know that. Their "maybe" expresses the perplexity of man's march through the world while waiting for the sole event of which everybody can be sure. One day Diego called for a truck and delivered the tree to the Odéon. There it stood for the run of the play, an eerie presence in the drama of man's isolation and loneliness.

Tom F. Driver

I asked what he thinks about those who find a religious significance to his plays.

"Well, really there is none at all. I have no religious feeling. Once I had a religious emotion. It was at my first Communion. No more. My mother was deeply religious. So was my brother. He knelt down at his bed as long as he could kneel. My father had none. The family was Protestant, but for me it was only irksome and I let it go. My brother and mother got no value from their religion when they died. At the moment of crisis it had no more depth than an old-school tie. Irish Catholicism is not attractive, but it is deeper. When you pass a church on an Irish bus, all the hands flurry in the sign of the cross. One day the dogs of Ireland will do that too and perhaps also the pigs."

But do the plays deal with the same facets of experience religion must also deal with?

"Yes, for they deal with distress. Some people object to this in my writing. At a party an English intellectual—so-called—asked me why I write always about distress. As if it were perverse to do so! He wanted to know if my father had beaten me or my mother had run away from home to give me an unhappy childhood. I told him no, that I had had a very happy childhood. Then he thought me more perverse than ever. I left the party as soon as possible and got into a taxi. On the glass partition between me and the driver were three signs: one asked for

From Tom F. Driver, "Beckett by the Madeleine," *Columbia University Forum* (1961); 21–25. Reprinted in *Samuel Beckett: The Critical Heritage*; eds. Lawrence Grover and Raymond Federman (London: Routledge & Kegan Paul, 1979). Reprinted by permission of Tom F. Driver.

help for the blind, another help for orphans, and the third for relief for the war refugees. One does not have to look for distress. It is screaming at you even in the taxis of London."

Deirdre Bair

He submitted his resignation [from the Red Cross] effective in January, 1946, but before it was accepted, he was called upon for one more service. Matron Mary Crowley, who had not been able to travel with the other Irish staff members the previous August, was due to arrive in Dieppe harbor in the early morning hours of Christmas Eve, aboard the *Isle of Thanet*, a converted coastal vessel now put into rescue service.[1] Beckett was asked to meet her.

The ship docked in the midst of a severe coastal storm that dropped many feet of snow on northern France. Beckett had driven through the storm from Paris in a Red Cross jeep, intent on driving Matron Crowley the two hundred miles to St. Lô before dawn on Christmas day. There was very little conversation because he had to concentrate on the driving, which was perilous. They drove through the snow, avoiding craters in the road and abandoned vehicles. Many bridges were blown up, necessitating frequent detours through minefields. Beckett drove on relentlessly, stopping only twice during the ten-hour drive. The first time was at a little cafe in a now forgotten village, where he disappeared briefly and reappeared carrying a steaming soup bowl filled with coffee laced with cognac. Matron Crowley, though famished and freezing, refused it, saying she "never took spirits." "Well you've got to now," Beckett insisted. "You can't get a thing to eat here—all the gold in the world wouldn't buy a piece of bread today in this area." She drank it without another word.

They arrived in St. Lô just as midnight Mass was starting. The snow, which had fallen inside the bombed-out, roofless cathedral, was frozen hard, glistening like white satin on the floor. The sky had cleared and was full of stars. On either side of the congregation, mines were piled up against the still-standing walls. Three very old men played violins while the congregation sang hymns with deep emotion. The only intact portion of the cathdral was the altar of the Virgin Mary, and enough

From Deirdre Bair, *Samuel Beckett* (New York: Harcourt, Brace, Jovanovich, 1978), 344–45. Reprinted by permission of Simon and Schuster.

[1]The following information is from Matron Mary Crowley, Dublin, November 4, 1974.

candles had been gathered by the villagers to light it brightly. On the fringe of the candlelight, the ruins gleamed in the ghostly shadows. Beckett stood stiffly while Matron Crowley knelt and prayed. She sensed his discomfort and spared him her verbal gratitude when the Mass was ended. Afterward he took her directly to her hospital quarters and then commandeered a bed for himself for a few hours' sleep. Early the next morning, when she tried to find him to thank him, Matron Crowley was told that he had gone back to Paris before dawn.

Beckett was not through with St. Lô yet. Matron Crowley was put in charge of all the nurses in all the wards. As the civilian populace returned in ever increasing numbers, the hospital began to fill up. There were wards for medical, surgical and ophthalmic patients. German prisoners who were well enough worked in the hospital, but the sick ones were patients until they recovered enough to help. Even the military sent patients. The French, British and Americans had all established hospitals of their own in the sectors under their control, but many of their patients were shunted off to the Irish. The greatest problem came from the maternity and children's wards, which were especially vulnerable to the rats and other vermin that roamed throughout the ruined town. It was virtually impossible to find chemical controls since none of the occupying armies had any to spare. Beckett was asked to do what he could: a hurried telephone call came to Paris asking him to find something to kill the rats. He went to friends at the Curie Hospital Department of Pathology—friends he had met through Péron—and they gave him a solution to put on bits of corncob which were scattered around the wards in strategic places where the rats ate them and then crawled away to die.

It was the last service he performed before his resignation took effect. Somehow it was a fitting one—the new year had begun with a triumph, new life over pestilence and death. He left the poison with Matron Crowley and hurried off to Paris for the last time, without waiting around to know the results. Killing rats was his last personal act of warfare.

Tom Dardis

The most notable of the films made in Keaton's last years was Samuel Beckett's *Film*, directed by Alan Schneider. Buster had been given

From Tom Dardis, *Keaton: The Man Who Wouldn't Lie Down* (New York: Penguin Books, 1980), 268–71. Reprinted by permission of Tom Dardis.

Waiting for Godot to read some years before, but turned it down because he didn't understand it. *Film* had been written for the Irish actor Jack MacGowran, who had agreed to take the role, but at the last moment he turned it down to accept an important part in Tony Richardson's *Tom Jones*. *Film* was being produced by Barney Rosset's Evergreen Films, and there was a great deal of debate as to who should replace MacGowran. It was Beckett who thought of Keaton, and Alan Schneider was dispatched to visit him in Woodland Hills with a copy of the script. Buster read it and was just as doubtful about *Film* as he had been about *Waiting for Godot,* but he accepted the offer of $5,000 for what amounted to two weeks' shooting in New York.

Alan Schneider was concerned about Buster's health and the potentially harmful effect on him of the heat of the New York streets. But there were no problems and Buster carried out his tasks energetically. Beckett had come to the United States for the first time to see the shooting of his script. At the end of each day's work he was driven back to Barney Rosset's house in the Hamptons, totally unwilling to meet his many admirers in the city. He did come around to see Buster at his hotel just before the shooting began, in his usual corner suite at the St. Moritz, and it was here that the two first met. Beckett proved to be as shy as Buster, and they had very little to say to each other.

Film called for Boris Kaufman's camera to follow Buster through the streets from the rear so that we never see his face. Various people in the street gasp in horror as they catch a glimpse of the man coming toward them. Buster arrives at the building where he lives and enters his apartment. He immediately shoos his cat and dog from the room and covers up the goldfish bowl so that its occupant cannot see him: *no one* must see him. After tearing up his family pictures, Buster is finally trapped by the camera; his expression of sheer living horror is frighteningly well done. The picture has found few supporters, many finding it a freakish tour de force, but there is a terrible urgency about the film; the fact that you know that the figure up there on the screen with his face hidden is Buster Keaton helps establish the strangeness that Beckett wanted to achieve. Buster himself did not care for the film, but his explanation as to "what it all meant" was as good as anyone else's: "What I think it means is that a man can keep away from everybody, but he can't get away from himself."

Buster had lunch every day with Beckett, Schneider, and the whole crew during those two weeks in June 1964. A number of scenes were shot on the Upper West Side, in the 140s, near the Hudson River. At a nearby restaurant Buster would hold forth on the great days in the twenties when he had his own production unit and made films like *The Navigator* and *The General*. Yet there was no trace of defeat or sadness in his manner. Beckett would listen intently to Buster's stories, a small smile of pure delight on his face.

Madeleine Renaud

Before playing *Oh! Les Beaux Jours (Happy Days)* I liked Beckett's work, and ever since I have admired the man, although he intimidates me.

First of all, he is very handsome, with a fascinating charm of which it seems to me he is unaware. And then, naturally, he is intelligent and subtle, possessing a rare tact and courtesy. When he came to Paris for rehearsals, he asked me: "Would it upset you if I helped you with your part?" Usually authors insist on it, and they are right to do so.

For two months Roger Blin, Beckett and I worked together in the empty, silent halls of the Odéon. We learned every word by heart, every speech in the most absolute confidence. Yes, Beckett showed complete confidence in Roger Blin and myself. He was always there, terribly present and yet silent. Once, when a certain passage was giving me trouble, he said to me: "But, if it worries you, it must be cut!" Coming from an author, it was a very rare phrase indeed. And as he possesses a sense of theatre to an astonishing degree, the sense of creating an effect, we also accorded him an equal confidence.

I can say that those two months of rehearsal were very rich for me. First of all as an actress—I have a long career behind me, and yet Blin and Beckett opened a completely new window onto my career. And then too as a woman. Certainly my contacts with Beckett were difficult: he speaks very little, never makes confidences, never allows himself to be taken by surprise; he only reveals himself through his writings; and he never comes to performances of his plays because he cannot bear to find himself in direct contact with the public. Does this mean that he despises them? I do not think so, but rather that he suffers from extreme embarrassment.

Who knows Beckett? Undoubtedly his wife does. But as for others, for myself? I only know what he looks like.

We worked together for two months, in total confidence; he came to

From Madeleine Renaud, "Beckett the Magnificent," in *Beckett at 60* (London: Calder & Boyars, 1967), 81–83. Reprinted by permission of John Calder.

dinner several times at my house, and it was certainly not from a desire to be social. But I have never been to where he lives and I do not possess any photograph of him. From time to time he sends me a card. That is all.

But all the same, I know that he thinks of me as a friend and that this friendship is loyal; I have the proof of it. A film director (why not name him, it was Jean-Luc Godard) asked him for permission to film *Oh! Les Beaux Jours*. Beckett refused and replied that he could not envisage *Oh! Les Beaux Jours* without Madeleine Renaud. Authors, where their interest is concerned, do not often feel themselves committed to their interpreters to this extent. But Beckett is more than an author, he is a poet. Above all, a profoundly sincere man, as sincere as he is secret. He cannot bear the symbols that are found in his work, the theories that are elaborated out of his writings. When I say "he cannot bear" I mean that he wants to ignore them, because I have never seen him in a rage. In any case, he refuses to be defined as a twentieth-century author, the head of an avant-garde. I think that he simply wants to be a man who knows how to observe and to understand. The universe that he describes is certainly his own, he lives it every day, and for him it is descriptive evidence itself.

One could work twenty hours a day with Beckett without ever seeing him relax or depart from his reserve. The best way to understand him is to read his works without looking for any philosophy other than a great human compassion. *Oh! Les Beaux Jours* is a marvellous love poem, the song of a woman who still wants to see and hear the man she loves. When I read the play for the first time I was overcome by it. I was reading everything that I had not dared to think since . . . since my first middle-aged wrinkle. And how quickly those wrinkles come!

It can seem cruel to play a Winnie, just as it can be cruel to cast any lucid glance on the human condition. It is true that no-one can go farther than *Oh! Les Beaux Jours*. At any rate, I do not think so.

I do not know what Beckett thinks of women, but I know that he understands them profoundly from the inside. If his plays manage to affect us and move us (and if they did not succeed in invading our sensibilities they would not be played throughout the entire world), it is because Beckett, in spite of his modesty, manages to express his immense compassion for all human life and because he is one of those exceptional men to whom love and lucidity are on the same level.

THE CRITICS

Introduction

Though critics were at first slow to appreciate their potential, the plays, novels, and stories of Samuel Beckett have for 25 years now nourished a full-blown "Beckett industry" in academic circles. Books by the score and articles by the hundreds have already appeared, with no end or even abatement in sight. The *Journal of Beckett Studies* exists in support of the cause.

This vast exploration has left few paths unexplored, but it seems a fair generalization to suggest that critics have interested themselves especially in Beckett's apparent formal innovations and/or his literary and philosophical sources. The latter explorations were encouraged by the fact that the early poem *Whoroscope* featured Descartes as its speaker and *Murphy* and *More Pricks than Kicks* deployed thinkers as famous as Heraclitus and Democritus and as obscure as Hippasos and Arnold Geulincx. The studies of formal innovations were fueled by such modern and postmodern sophistications as comic footnotes (though these reminded traditionalists of Swift or Sterne), apparent scorn for conventions of plot and character, and derision especially for himself, for his own efforts, his own creations. That the author reserved his strongest expressions of esteem for Dante and Synge and insisted on his ignorance of philosophy has deterred no one.

The studies included here were selected and edited for their coherent focus on a specific short work. Accessibility of style was as important as it could be, given the primary goal. Last and least, but still significant, is a bias in favor of more recent pieces. Important earlier studies, and others less susceptible to editing, are cited in the bibliography.

Rubin Rabinovitz

In its original version *More Pricks than Kicks* had not ten but eleven stories. However, an editor at Chatto and Windus (the firm that was about to publish Beckett's novel) decided that the last story, "Echo's Bones," should be dropped.[1] "Echo's Bones" has never appeared in print: the shortened version was used for all subsequent editions of the novel. It is easy to imagine why Beckett's editor—no doubt motivated by the best intentions—found the story objectionable. The setting is unrealistic, the plot improbable, the characters bizarre. The narrator's urbane conceits give way to thighslappers of a lower order (like a joke about an ostrich named Strauss who simply waltzes along). Even the costumes are outlandish: a cemetery groundsman, clad only in truss and boots, has a tattoo with the motto "Stultum Propter Christum" on his stomach.[2]

At the beginning of the story Belacqua—dead, buried, and in most quarters forgotten—makes a return appearance. He may have given up the ghost, but he retains many bad habits—picking his nose in the presence of ladies, for example. He has acquired a taste for cigars, and a stock of them. Death has deprived him of his shadow, and he can no longer see his reflection in a mirror. But he is still a self-centered snob with a love for abstruse conversation.

The narrator presents three episodes as representative examples of Belacqua's postmortem activities. The first one begins with Belacqua sitting on a fence, deep in meditation. Suddenly Zaborovna Privet, an alluring woman with a taste for "sublime delinquencies," emerges from a nearby hedge (Privet from hedge: another thighslapper). Zaborovna introduces herself to Belacqua and, after a long exchange of erudite banter, invites him home. The prospect of collaborating in her sublime delinquencies leaves him cold, but when Zaborovna offers him fried garlic and Cuban rum, he lets himself be persuaded. (Death, so inhib-

From "Learning to Live with Death: Echo's Bones," in *The Development of Samuel Beckett's Fiction* (Urbana: University of Illinois Press, 1984), 55–57, 59–61. Reprinted by permission of University of Illinois Press and Rubin Rabinovitz.

itory to other pleasures, has left Belacqua with an enhanced appreciation of olfactory sensations.) The garlic is prepared, consumed, washed down with rum, but when Zaborovna tries to embrace Belacqua, he vanishes. She is left alone with nothing but "the dream of the shadow of the smoke of a rotten cigar" (p. 7).

The next episode begins with a pensive Belacqua again sitting on a fence. His meditations are interrupted when he feels a sharp pain in his back—Belacqua has been hit by a golf ball. Its owner approaches, putter in hand. He is Lord Gall of Wormwood: landowner, connoisseur, raconteur, inventor; a man of gigantic proportions, distinguished lineage, and unparalleled athletic skill. One tragic circumstance makes Lord Gall as bitter as his name suggests.[3] Because he is childless and impotent, his estate will eventually revert to the Baron Extravas, his archenemy. Not only is the baron degenerate, evil-hearted, reptilian, and a bounder, but the syphilitic condition of Moll, Lord Gall's wife, can be attributed to him.

Lord Gall, his paternal instincts aroused, asks to be permitted to call his new acquaintance Adeodatus (after St. Augustine's illegitimate son). He then takes Belacqua to his aerie, a crow's nest on a great tree, and after a long exchange of recondite discourse proposes that Belacqua father a child on his behalf. The mercurial Belacqua, so recently a fugitive from Zaborovna's embraces, agrees. Unworried about hygienic complications ensuing from Moll's unfortunate illness, he joins Lord Gall on his mount (Strauss, the ostrich) and they gallop off. Belacqua meets Moll, whom he finds boring and repulsive; spends the night with her nevertheless; and proves to be remarkably virile, for a dead man. The episode, until now a blend of fairy tale, dream, and myth, ends as a shaggy-dog story. Moll becomes pregnant, but—alas for Lord Gall and his hopes for an heir—she gives birth to a girl.

Belacqua is again seated at the beginning of the last episode, not on a fence this time but on his own headstone. He encounters a character from "Draff," the cemetery groundsman who introduced the fable of the roses and the gardener. Now the groundsman is given a name, Doyle, as well as the striking truss-and-boots costume mentioned earlier. Doyle carries with him a considerable assortment of tools; as he explains, he plans to steal Belacqua's corpse. Belacqua assures him that such an endeavor would be pointless: he himself is the body. Doyle, however, ignores this as so much hocus-pocus. It may be that he is conversing with the spiritual remnant of Belacqua, but he nevertheless has every expectation of finding the corporal residue in the grave. Belacqua proposes that they bet on the question. After a long, arcane conversation Doyle accepts the bet and they dig down to the coffin and open it. Inside they find a handful of stones.

This incident (as the title, "Echo's Bones," hints) refers to one Ovid describes in the *Metamorphoses*: when Echo is spurned by Narcissus, she wastes away until her bones turn into stone. Nothing remains but her voice; because her chatter once distracted Juno, she is condemned to repeat the last thing she hears. Echo, like many of the figures in the *Metamorphoses*, must endure a form of retribution appropriate to her misdeeds. Belacqua's punishment is based on a similar idea. His conversation has annoyed others; now he cannot remain silent. Once he urged his fiancée to take a lover; in the afterlife he becomes the lover of another man's wife. The narcissistic Belacqua can no longer see his face in a mirror; this, he says, is more agonizing "than all the other pains and aches of the reversion" (p. 13). His expiation, says the narrator, will improve Belacqua: he will become "a trifle better, dryer, less of a natural snob" (p. 1). The drying process leaves Belacqua dessicated, and finally his physical remains, like Echo's, turn into stone. . . .

In the *Metamorphoses* Echo suffers because she has been spurned; Narcissus, because he cannot embrace his reflected image. Belacqua's unhappiness is related to both dilemmas: Echo represents his need to love another, and Narcissus stands for his inability to give of himself. Love is demanding; narcissism is unrewarding; Belacqua shuttles between these extremes and is left emotionally drained. By the end of the story he is more like Echo than like Narcissus, so parched and shriveled that he is little more than a voice and some stones.

In *Dream of Fair to Middling Women* Beckett used a similar technique—again involving figures from Ovid—to illustrate Belacqua's inner conflicts.[4] There, three aspects of Belacqua's personality are described: "Centripetal, centrifugal and . . . not. Phoebus chasing Daphne, Narcissus fleeing from Echo and . . . neither."[5] Phoebus Apollo represents Belacqua's unfulfilled need for love (Apollo, like Echo, has been rejected). Narcissus again represents the self-involvement that prevents Belacqua from giving of himself. A third category ("neither") negates the first two, and indicates that Belacqua's psychological state is too complex to be defined by a simple antithesis.

In "Echo's Bones" there is no third category; instead, the recurring details are used to enhance the complexity of the narrator's characterization of Belacqua. The most obvious of the recurring elements is a

The Critics

reiterated passage of over one hundred words that appears first in "Draff" and then in "Echo's Bones." The length of the passage (a description of the view from the cemetery where Belacqua is buried) indicates that the inclusion of recurring elements in the novel is not careless but intentional.[6]

Beckett's technique resembles one Ovid uses in the *Metamorphoses*. Though Echo is forced to repeat the last thing she hears, her remarks are not nonsensical. The speeches of Narcissus end with phrases that, when Echo utters them, express her own feelings. The following passage is an example:

> "Keep your hands off," he cried, "and do not touch me!
> I would die before I give you a chance at me."
> "I give you a chance at me," and that was all
> She ever said thereafter. . . .[7]

Beckett's echo device is based on a similar principle: the repeated phrases take on a new meaning in a different context. When Belacqua tells Winnie he wants to go off by himself for "sursum corda," the excuse seems plausible; when he later gives Lucy the same excuse, his sincerity is called into question.[8] Other repeated passages emphasize inconsistencies that reveal Belacqua's contradictory impulses: his desire to become involved in a relationship, and his desire to run away.

Ostensibly the narrator identifies only with the narcissistic side of Belacqua: he condones Belacqua's behavior and conceals his faults. But like Belacqua (who is in a sense his alter ego), the narrator has a trait that makes him comparable to Echo: he keeps repeating things.[9] The narrator may pretend that Belacqua is no more than an insensitive egotist, but the recurring passages illuminate the more vulnerable side of Belacqua's personality. The Narcissus theme is emphasized in the content, and depicts Belacqua's mask; the Echo theme is hinted at by the formal devices that suggest what lies behind the mask. In this way Beckett ingeniously preserves a union of form and content.

Notes

1. Deirdre Bair, *Samuel Beckett: A Biography* (New York: Harcourt Brace Jovanovich, 1978), p. 162. Bair mentions that the deletion of the story provoked Beckett to write a poem with the title "Echo's Bones"; see pp. 663–64n. The poem appeared in *Echo's Bones and other Precipitates*, published in 1935.

2. "Echo's Bones" (TS, Dartmouth College Library), p. 20. Subsequent page references to "Echo's Bones" in this chapter are to the Dartmouth type-script. I am grateful to the authorities of the Dartmouth College Library for making this source accessible. The Latin motto "Stultum Propter Christum" means "On Account of a Foolish Christ." It may be, however, that "Stultum" is a misprint for "Stultus"; if so, the phrase would mean "A Fool on Account of Christ." On the same page Beckett speaks of the groundsman as "a sweet dolt on some Christ's account." The "fool on account of Christ" idea, which appears in the writings of Erasmus, Jacopone da Todi, and others, can be traced back to I Corinthians 4:10 ("We are fools for Christ's sake . . ."). I am grateful to my colleague Richard J. Schoeck for pointing out the source of this allusion.

3. The name is from the Bible, where wormwood and gall are mentioned together to epitomize bitterness. See Deuteronomy 29:18, Jeremiah 9:15, 23:15, and Lamentations 3:19.

4. Beckett may have been influenced by Joyce, who used a similar de-vice. In *A Portrait of the Artist as a Young Man* Stephen thinks of himself as a young Daedalus, but at the very end of the book he hints that he may also be the son of Daedalus. A second reading of the novel reveals other connections between Stephen and Icarus, and leads to another way of interpreting the ac-tion. Like Stephen, Belacqua is linked with two mythical figures whose story is told in the *Metamorphoses*, and the figures represent antithetical aspects of his personality.

5. *Dream of Fair to Middling Women* (TS, Dartmouth College Library), p. 107. The passage I have quoted is complete; the ellipses are in the original. The Apollo and Daphne story is in Book I of the *Metamorphoses*. In his essay on *Finnegans Wake* Beckett mentions Vico's idea that "every need of life, nat-ural, moral and economic, has its verbal expression in one or other of the 30,000 Greek divinities. This is Homer's 'language of the Gods'"; see "Dante . . . Bruno . Vico . . Joyce," in *Our Exagmination Round his Factifica-tion for Incamination of Work in Progress* (1929; rpt., London: Faber and Faber, 1972), p. 10. By using Ovid's figures to represent psychological forces, Beckett is illustrating a way of applying Vico's idea.

6. The passage, which describes the actions of the cemetary grounds-man, begins, "What with the company of headstones . . ." and ends with "He sang a little song . . . ," *More Pricks than Kicks* (1934; rpt., New York: Grove Press, 1970), pp. 190–91. The corresponding passage (on p. 19 of "Echo's Bones") describes the actions of Belacqua and not the groundsman. This sug-gests that the groundsman—like some of the other characters in the book—may be an alter ego of Belacqua's, a portion of himself that attends the burial of another part.

7. Ovid, p. 69 (Book III, II. 390ff).

8. *More Pricks than Kicks*, pp. 29, 107.

9. A suggestion that Belacqua represents the narrator's alter ego comes when he calls Belacqua "my little intermus homo"; *More Pricks than Kicks*, p. 38.

S. Jean Walton

"First Love" (written in 1946, published in 1970 in French and in 1974 in English), offers us a particularly revealing imaging of Beckett's perception of expression as a kind of extortion. The only one of the early first-person narratives which was not published until much later, it is also the only story to link the split from the father to a union with a female Other. Only here is the protagonist so explicitly portrayed as flanked by his previous role as son and his potential role (via his union with Lulu) as father. In "First Love," the process of extortion in which a story, meaning, or narrative is twisted out of the writer finds its corollary in a kind of sexual extortion, where sperm is forced out of the unwilling protagonist. In this way, the story begins to address the question that preoccupies Beckett in all his writings: how one gets from the self as son, as lover, as potential father (*living* what he is called on to "express") to the self which is a self-proclaimed writer, who exists not prior to but by virtue of his own writing. . . .

"First Love" is the story of a protagonist's banishment, after the death of his father, from the house where he has been more or less contentedly inanimate, and his subsequent union with a woman who produces in him the state of love. The "plot" of the story begins only after the father's death; prior to this death the protagonist's own life is not yet narratable, since his father is the protector of his stasis in the family abode and guarantees that he will not be displaced from it.

To understand *why* the prenarratable existence in the shelter of the father's house would be so desirable, it might help to contrast it to the *un*desirable state of sexual arousal, which in this story follows almost as a consequence of the father's death. When the father is no longer

From "Extorting Love's Tale from the Banished Son: Origins of Narratability in Samuel Beckett's 'First Love,'" *Contemporary Literature* 29 (1988): 549–63. Reprinted by permission of *Contemporary Literature*.

alive to extend protection, the protagonist, expelled from the house, is exposed to the disturbances of a female Other and finds himself "at the mercy of an erection." "On such occasions," he says, "One is no longer oneself . . . and it is painful to be no longer oneself, even more painful if possible than when one is. For when one is one knows what to do to be less so, whereas when one is not one is any old one irredeemably" (18). It is not that the protagonist wants to *be himself* so much as that he wants to control the way in which he becomes less himself. As we recall from Freud, the goal of life is not merely death, which would be an easy matter, given the myriad life-threatening agents among which the living being wanders, but in fact one's very own individual death, the death which waits at the end of one's "own path" and not at the end of a diverging "circuitous path." In the father's house, then, the protagonist presumably still has control over how to be "less" himself, how to die in his own fashion.

It would seem then that the father is on the side of the "organism," as the protector of the right to die in its own fashion. But to *become* a father is to become one of those forces "of whose nature we can form no conception" and, by engendering new life, to induce another "inanimate organism" to diverge from its stasis. The narrator of "First Love" thinks that it is his father who has protected him for all those years, so that he would be left alone in his house. In fact, it was his father who brought him into the world in the first place, and whose death occasions a second rude expulsion when the narrator is thrown out of the house.

In addition, the narrator assumes at first that he has been expelled against his father's last wishes. But his opinion is amended by a semi-ironic afterthought: "Poor Papa, a nice mug he must have felt that day if he could see me, see us, a nice mug on my account I mean. Unless in his great disembodied wisdom he saw further than his son whose corpse was not yet quite up to scratch" (16). In other words, perhaps the son's expulsion is within the intentions of the father after all, in an overall plan which the protagonist cannot understand from his perspective as an unfinished corpse. No corpse is "up to scratch" until it is finally dead. The living are corpses in the making, as yet incomplete, unripe, raw. The father has reached the state of "great disembodied wisdom." The son strives toward it. And the thought which has occurred to him here is the possibility that his ejection from the house is a necessary step in his attainment of the goal of stasis as a corpse.

Set on his wanderings, the protagonist meets with another force that disturbs him even more than his ejection from the house. This is of course Lulu, whose presence causes an erection in him and, subsequently, the state of love. That this constitutes a disturbance of stasis is evidenced by his acerbic comment about love: "What goes by the name of love is banishment, with now and then a postcard from the homeland, such is my considered opinion, this evening" (18). Banished from himself by the disturbance wrought on him by sexual desire, he wishes only that his "self" be "resumed, mine own, the mitigable" (18).

What is emphasized in the first meeting between the protagonist and Lulu is the unexpectedness of her irruption into his life. He takes pains to describe the temporary haven he has found for himself on the bench by the canal, how it affords him protection by virtue of its semihidden location. It is a "well situated bench" in this respect, and "the risk of surprise was small. And yet she surprised me" (16–17). His sense of protected security is suddenly violated: his attempt to re-create as best he can the insularity of his room in the house, and his supineness of body and mind, is thwarted by this appearance of an Other that takes him by surprise.

"Surprise" might best be understood as a screen word used to deflect attention from what really underlies the narrator's fear and vulnerability. When the narrator is brought to tears, for instance, it is not, he assures us, because he feels sorrow. Rather it is because he has "caught sight of something unbeknownst" (24). Though he stresses that it is the element of surprise that makes him weep and not the nature of the object that has surprised him, one tends to suspect that certain things affect, indeed frighten him more than others. Insisting that he "feels nothing" in Lulu's presence, for instance, he reports that the sight of her "hands buried in a muff" brings tears to his eyes (24). This remark is followed immediately by a rationalization and a denial of the muff's power to move him: if things caught sight of "unbeknownst" are what make him cry, he says, perhaps he is wrong to have singled out this *particular* thing: "So I wonder if it was really the muff that evening, if it was not rather the path, so iron hard and bossy as perhaps to feel like cobbles to my tread, or some other thing, some chance thing glimpsed below the threshold, that so unmanned me" (24). It is no coincidence that his crying, as expressive of his emotion, is imaged as an "unmanning," or a kind of castration, since the elaborate measures to discount

the importance of the muff serve in fact to emphasize its true significance. This exterior muff, this haven for Lulu's hands, is a reminder
to him of that other hidden muff which he has "glimpsed below the
threshold" of his consciousness and which he involuntarily seeks himself, being "at the mercy of an erection" (18). The prospect of finding
refuge in this hidden, unpredictable muff is a frightening one, the
source of his agitation, and it is that which, "unbeknownst" to him,
brings tears to his eyes, or "unmans" him. Indeed, from the moment
he meets Lulu and perceives his attraction to her, his reaction consists
of a series of various forms of denial. And what is most frequently denied, postponed, avoided is what, after all, occupies the most traumatic
position in the psyche.

Perhaps most indicative of the protagonist's sexual anxiety is his repeated procrastination about the consummation of this first love, particularly in the retrospective retelling of it. His report of the symptoms
by which he recognizes he has fallen in love is interrupted repeatedly
by digressions. Finally he acknowledges that he indulges in so many
"particulars" in order to "put off the evil hour" (26). If his text is over-
laden with what seem to be unnecessary digressions it is because he
wants to stave off the climax of his narrative for as long as possible. As
he gets closer to the "evil hour," he acknowledges his delay twice
more: after a fanciful sketch of Lulu's grandmother on her close-stool,
he remarks, "That's the idea, procrastinate" (30), and a few lines later,
in midsentence, "that's the idea, every particular" (30).

The procrastination in the writing repeats the protagonist's procrastination during the scene that leads up to the dreaded consummation.
After a series of attempts to rebuff Lulu's advances to him once they
enter her flat, he is faced by her frank question: "Will you not undress?" (28). His attempt to conceal his embarrassment and anxiety at
this point is almost touching in its limp bravado: "Oh you know, I said,
I seldom undress. It was the truth, I was never one to undress indis-
criminately. I often took off my boots when I went to bed, I mean when
I composed myself (composed!) to sleep, not to mention this or that
outer garment according to the outer temperature" (28).

He arranges a barricaded nest for himself by turning the sofa to the
wall and climbing into it "like a dog into its basket" (30). Finally,
clutching a stewpan in case he should need to relieve himself in the
night, and because it "reassures" him to have something in his hand
when sleeping, he settles down into his new haven, "alone at last, in

the dark at last" (30–31). But the consummation is to take place after all, in spite of all his panicked measures to forestall it.

What is interesting is that this union to which he has been so reluctantly leading happens off-stage, as it were, is too traumatic to be described in the text, as a memory expressed for the benefit of the reader; indeed, it is too traumatic even to be consciously experienced by the protagonist when it occurs: "I thought I was all set for a good night, in spite of the strange surroundings, but no, my night was most agitated. I woke next morning quite spent, my clothes in disorder, the blanket likewise, and Anna beside me, naked naturally. One shudders to think of her exertions. I still had the stewpan in my grasp. It had not served. I looked at my member. If only it could have spoken! Enough about that. It was my night of love" (31). What has been led up to here is a gap: in consciousness and in narrative, an empty spot where the climactic moment, or the "evil hour," should be. The union toward which this love has been yearning is jumped over and left behind.

But it has served its purpose, or rather two purposes: it has restored him to himself (if only temporarily), and extorted the sperm which will engender (if we are to believe Lulu) the next generation. . . .

At the end of the story, the "night of love" results in a pregnancy which soon makes the protagonist a reluctant father. "What finished me was the birth," he announces, in a conflation of opposites that once again links beginning to ending (35). This unwanted repetition of his own birth, this forcing out of a comfortably inactive, hitherto undisturbed organism, is attended by Lulu's cries, which force the protagonist from his nest: "There was no competing with those cries. It must have been her first. They pursued me down the stairs and out into the street" (35). Unlike her singing, these cries disturb the protagonist exceedingly, perhaps because of their extreme expressiveness: they are the heralds of something really inside Lulu that is literally going to come out. This birth is the ultimate pressing out of what is inside, the re-enactment of the narrator's own forced exit from his mother's womb.

Refusing to act out his role in the forward progression of the generative chain, the protagonist regresses once more to try, vainly, to reaffirm his tie to his father.[1] Having noted that he can still hear the distressing cries even outside the house and that he does not know where he is (being "banished" from familiar ground), he looks among the stars and constellations for the Wains but cannot find them without his father's help (35). The father is cut off for good, no longer "beside"

119

his son (because the son is "beside" himself), and so the son has no recourse but to try to manipulate Lulu's insistent cries in the same way he has attempted to manipulate her singing: "I began playing with the cries, a little in the same way as I had played with the song, on, back, on, back, if that may be called playing. As long as I kept walking I didn't hear them, because of the footsteps. But as soon as I halted I heard them again, a little fainter each time, admittedly, but what does it matter, faint or loud, cry is cry, all that matters is that it should cease" (35–36). He makes the cries appear and disappear, like the child's toy or his reflection in the mirror. The object of the game is not only to make the cries go away but to be certain that they really have stopped. The playing, however, merely gives him a temporary illusion that they have stopped; when he walks, the sound of his own footsteps masks, covers up, hides the sound of the cries. His own motion, his "walking," not only distances him from the source of his anguish but can replace that source with its own noise, just as the language of a text replaces the author that brought it into being and the tombstone covers up the corpse. The protagonist persists for "years" in this expedient, this attempt to silence the cries by his own footsteps, by his own forays into language: "For years I thought they would cease. Now I don't think so any more" (36). In other words, he still hears the cries, even as an old man; they constitute the "disturbance" that he has incorporated into his "winning" system, the "killing memories" that cannot be stamped out but at least enfeebled by constant repetition, by coaxing them to appear and disappear in between the paces of his footfalls, the traces of his words.

Note

1. Kristeva touches on this idea in her study: "Assumption of self through the dead father turns the banished writer into a father in spite of himself, a father under protest, a false father who doesn't want to be a father, but nevertheless believes in being one—tense in the elegance of permanent mourning" (151–52). The study cited is Julia Kristeva, "The Father, Love, and Banishment" in *Desire in Language: A Semiotic Approach to Literature and Art* (New York: Columbia University Press, 1980).

Brian Finney

Samuel Beckett's *Imagination Dead Imagine* is at once a powerful and beautiful piece of writing while being, one has to admit, appallingly difficult to understand. Undoubtedly much of this difficulty stems from the fact that it is a distillation of a longer work. To quote from the Calder and Boyars first English edition of 1966 (a translation by Beckett of *Imagination Morte Imaginez* published in 1965): "The present short work was conceived as a novel, started as a novel, and in spite of its brevity, remains a novel, a work of fiction from which the author has removed all but the essentials, having first imagined them and created them."

There is no point in getting involved in sterile arguments as to what constitutes a novel. The point that needs emphasizing is that the present text, consisting of some 1100 words, is a condensation of a much longer work. In this process of reduction many of the normal practices of prose writing on which the reader depends have been partially discarded: repetition (though his constant use of repetition—with modulations—in *Ping* doesn't make that work any easier to understand), syntax, punctuation—all operate in abbreviated form. Added to this is the frequent use of paradox—in the title and in such phrases as "No way in go in" or "from this point of view, but there is no other." There are even—one must assume, deliberate—inconsistencies: having created, for example, a monotone world, the left eyes of the figures are observed to be "piercing pale blue."

The net result of all this is a piece of fictional writing of perplexing obscurity—but of great beauty it seemed to me even on a first reading. I feel that sense can be made of this work, and once it has rendered its meaning, or as much of its meaning as is accessible, the meticulous craftsmanship that has gone into its composition becomes more apparent. As my intention is therefore to help the reader understand this work more fully, I make no apologies for offering next two diagrams—

From "A Reading of Beckett's *Imagination Dead Imagine*," *Twentieth Century Literature* 17 (1971): 65–71. Reprinted by Twentieth Century Literature.

a plan and an elevation—of the central image in *Imagination Dead Imagine*:

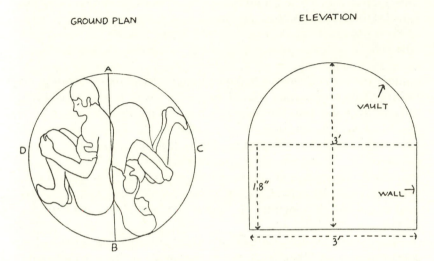

GROUND PLAN   ELEVATION

The most noticeable characteristic of this image is its concreteness. It is observed, described with the use of architectural and geometrical terminology, measured, felt. Variations from an empirically established norm are plotted meticulously. Simple scientific experiments (the mirror, the murmur in the silence) are conducted to test the response of the two bodies. This is to be no ordinary fictional image but a highly particularized set of phenomena scrutinised as objectively as is permissible since the theory of relativity became commonplace.

I think it is worth pointing out this early how much of the work is written in pseudo-scientific language. For much of it Beckett has attempted to strip all emotive connotations from his bare statements of descriptive fact (e.g. "Diameter three feet, three feet from ground to summit of the vault"). And it is also worth noting his failure to achieve complete objectivity, a failure he is aware of, as I hope to demonstrate later. An example of this "failure" is the attempt of scientific impersonality in the observation of the two figures: "the bodies seem whole and in fairly good condition, to judge by the surfaces exposed to view"—the effect is surely meant to be comical and focuses attention on the increasing difficulty facing the would-be objective narrator.

But to return to the nature of the central image: where, one asks, does it originate? The answer lies in the first three sentences. In the first of the three, the reader is told that only when his imagination is dead will he be able to see a "trace of life." Paradoxically once his imagination is dead, he is told to imagine. There are however two possible readings here: either a distinction is being made between two different kinds of imagination (implied by the paradox), a conventionally conceived imagination which can at its greatest conjure up Shakespeare's "cloud-capped towers" or Wordsworth's "sounding cataract," and a totally different imaginative faculty that deals with scientifically observed and measured-impossibilities; or he is telling the reader: imagine that your imagination is dead. Either way the second sentence describes naturalistic images which belong to the kind of imagination which the reader has been told to discard. It is interesting that these include natural phenomena as opposed to the rotunda and colours as opposed to the monotones that belong to the vision of "all white in the whiteness the rotunda" which can only be seen by a deadening of normal imagination.

But with the next sentence—"No way in, go in, measure"—the perplexing contradictoriness of this object of the non-imaginative vision is underlined. A rotunda without an entrance, it can yet be entered and measured with great exactitude, although its dimension will hardly leave room for a third adult, even when bent double! All the measurements, observations and experiments are surely intended to stress the actuality of the rotunda and its occupants: this is real, this is true, this is solid as bone—or at least as bone when rapped would sound *in the imagination*. And yet the reader can go through the solid walls which themselves disappear in the surrounding whiteness as soon as one moves back or up.

Once more the deliberate use of paradox is best understood by comparison to Shakespeare's world of the poetic imagination which turns out to consist of a "baseless fabric" which will "dissolve" and "leave not a rack behind." Beckett appears to be positing an imaginative construct which is the alter ego of Shakespeare's: only reached by a denial of normal imagination, this rotunda and its occupants are of far more durable stuff—if only one could keep its image before one. It will withstand all those scientific criteria before which Shakespeare's "gorgeous palaces" and "solemn temples" wither for lack of substantiality (how many palaces? how large? of what does "gorgeous" consist? etc.). But as with so many of the definitions of the scientist, one can never be rid of the part played by the human, oh-so-fallible observer. Here lies the rub.

123

Beckett has shown his allegiance to the rationalist school of philosophy since at least 1930 when he chose Descartes for his hero in *Whoroscope*. As he puts it in his book on *Proust* (1931): "the individual is a succession of individuals; the world being a projection of the individual's consciousness (an objectification of the individual's will, Schopenhauer would say), the pact must be continually renewed, the letter of safe-conduct brought up to date. The creation of the world did not take place once and for all time, but takes place every day." It is this conceptualist or Occasionalist view of existence (a view still offered by the hero of *How it Is*) which explains why Beckett regards it as miraculous that, after losing sight of the image in the temporary calm of the black dark, it should return at all, and also why it can never be entirely the same image as before: "Rediscovered miraculously after what absence in perfect voids it is no longer quite the same, from this point of view, but there is no other."

This is what makes the narrator's increasingly desperate attempts to observe and define the image with accuracy appear more and more absurd, pitiful and funny. By the time we reach such pseudo-objective observations as: "The faces too, assuming the two sides of a piece, seem to want nothing essential" we are forced to laugh at the preposterous scrupulosity of the narrator. His efforts at eliminating the subjectivity of the human observer's viewpoint only serve to underline the impossibility of getting at the image except through such an observer.

Rosemary Pountney

According to Beckett, *Sans/Lessness* was written in French "about 1969" and first appeared in English in the *New Statesman* of 1 May 1970. The piece was composed with astonishing precision and remains unique among Beckett's works in that he later produced a "key" to its construction, which enables a reader to disentangle the separate elements of which it is constituted. The key also makes it possible to reassemble

From "The Structuring of *Lessness*," *Review of Contemporary Fiction* 7 (1987): 55–75. Reprinted by permission of *Review of Contemporary Fiction*.

these elements into a new form, using Beckett's own method of arrangement.

Lessness is composed of sixty sentences, divided into six sections of ten sentences each. These are lettered by Beckett A 1–10, B 1–10, C 1–10, D 1–10, E 1–10, and F 1–10, but they do not appear in the text in this order. Instead, the sentences are shuffled into a completely different order and formed into twelve paragraphs containing varying numbers of sentences. The entire process is then repeated. Each sentence appears once more in a different order and paragraph sequence which forms the second half of the text. The complete work thus consists of 120 sentences divided into 24 paragraphs.[1]

Ruby Cohn relates that Beckett described to her how the final arrangement of sentences was achieved:

> Beckett wrote each of these sixty sentences on a separate piece of paper, mixed them all in a container, and then drew them out in random order twice. This became the order of the hundred twenty sentences in *Sans*. Beckett then wrote the number 3 on four separate pieces of paper, the number 4 on six pieces of paper, the number 5 on four pieces, the number 6 on six pieces, and the number 7 on four pieces of paper. Again drawing randomly, he ordered the sentences into paragraphs according to the number drawn, finally totally one hundred twenty.[2]

Beckett told Cohn this was "the only honest thing to do." The random method, known as aleatory technique (dependent on the throw of a die), has been used by composers to establish the order in which numbered bars of music should be placed. It is illustrated, for example, in *Musikalisches Wüfelspiel*, attributed to Mozart (K.Anh.C.30.01) which shows how an unlimited number of waltzes, rondos, hornpipes and reels could be composed according to the throw of a die, and a similar principle governs John Cage's *Music of Changes* for piano (1951).

That Beckett placed his highly formal, carefully patterned work at hazard in this way aptly illustrates his view of the human condition. Beyond the man-made or imposed order, Beckett seems to be saying, lies an arbitrary and capricious world of chance. The same kind of statement occurs at the beginning of *Murphy*, where the novelist spends some time enumerating the knots tying Murphy to his chair, but the unpredictable happens and the result of his calculations is wrong. Although Beckett may well be enjoying a joke here at the expense of the Cartesian faith in mathematical truth, he is also demonstrating the fallibility of supposed certainties. Murphy might be assumed to have no head for figures but it may be observed that in *All That Fall*, Mr. Rooney, who is devoted to mathematics ("one of the few satisfactions in life!") encounters the same difficulty. He attempts to count the station steps, but can never arrive at a fixed number. "Sometimes I wonder if they do not change them in the night."[3] Behind the world of apparently logical relations Beckett shows us a state of things so arbitrary that man's continued strivings towards order are no more than a mockery. It is his blinkered presence in the cosmos, his steadfast refusal to confront the facts of his condition squarely (as with Winnie in *Happy Days*) that marks the peculiar irony of his existence.

There are three parts to the key to *Lessness*. Beckett writes out each sentence of the piece, labeling it with a particular letter and number from A 1–F 10. A separate sheet shows these sentences twice arranged in paragraph order. He finally includes an explanation (headed "Key") of the elements common to each group of sentences.[4] Although Beckett's key is necessary in order to establish any progression of thought in *Sans/Lessness*, the shuffled arrangement of sentences makes its own points by introducing the element of chance into formal patterning and, by emphasizing the cyclic nature of the piece, gives it its particular quality of endlessness. Instead of a prose statement in which certain themes evolve and some kind of progression from A 1–F 10 may be deduced, the themes become linked in paragraphs that lead nowhere. Each paragraph of interleaved statements forms its own small circle of thought and is thus held static. These circles in turn revolve round each other, within the circle formed by linked phrases in the first and last paragraphs, thus forming a tight, verselike structure.

When read consecutively from A 1–F 10, *Lessness* may be seen to be concerned with recurring time cycles. Beckett's choice of a cyclic mode of expression to state a circular idea seems to be an example of the union of form and content that he noticed with such enthusiasm in the work of Joyce.[5] In *Lessness*, the fact that the circles of words have been described as coming about fortuitously, comments upon the nature of time itself. Time is endless (hence the circles) but structured human time is arbitrary (hence the accidental arrangement of these circles). Cohn sums it up as follows:

> Though the text is almost bare of figures, it compels calculation, and the resultant numbers serve to call attention to human time. The number of sentences per paragraph stops at seven, the number

of days in a week. The number of paragraphs reaches twenty-four, the number of hours in a day. The number of different sentences is sixty, the number of seconds in a minute, of minutes in an hour. But the repetition of the sixty sentences in a different order suggests the capricious arrangement of passing time.[6]

Given that the arrangement of sentences is arbitrary, they seem almost uncannily well dispersed. Not only do the sentences appear deftly interwoven, but each paragraph seems complete in itself, and aptly to fit into the pattern of the whole. The statement in each paragraph can either stand alone or be seen as part of a pattern of recurring statements. This dual quality is partly due to the structure of each sentence, for there is no syntax apart from full stops. Each phrase, unpinned by commas, has the capacity to be part of the whole or to stand alone. As in *Ping*, from which, Beckett states in the key, *Lessness* "proceeds," there are no verbs. Thus phrases may be linked in the reader's mind by, for example, the present tense, as:

B 1 (It is) Ash Grey (on) all sides earth sky (are) as one
(on) all sides (there is) endlessness.

Such an exercise loses the poetic quality of the prose. It was precisely Beckett's intention to free the language from the weight of tense and make all the sentences multidimensional, thus:

A 8 (There were
(There are
Scattered ruins ash grey all sides true refuge
(There will be   long last issueless

Repetition permeates *Lessness*; not only repetition of phrases that, because of the shuffled arrangement, reverberate through the text, but onomatopoeic repetition, as in words echoing the title (endlessness, changelessness) or words approximating towards the title (timeless, issueless). The sounds "less" and "ness" thus become distinctly recognized notes as the text unfolds. Alliterative repetition of this kind is also an integral part of the original French text. "Sans" is echoed, for example, in "sanctuaire," "temps," "en," "blanc," "passant," "encore" and "silence."

Despite the element of chance in its construction *Lessness* appears precisely balanced. There is, for example, exact polarization in the language, in phrases such as old love/new love, other nights/better days, light white/blacked out. Color values themselves are balanced. Light and darkness is of course a recurring theme in Beckett's work; in *Lessness* the predominant color is grey, a merging of white and black that reflects the sameness and uniformity of the repetitive language and the blank world it describes:

A 9 Scattered ruins same grey as the sand ash grey true refuge.
B 6 No sound not a breath same grey all sides earth sky body ruins.

When, in this grey world, the color blue appears, the surprise effect parallels that of the "little body heart beating" that stands out the more sharply for its background of blank planes.

The effectiveness of *Lessness* rests on keeping a balance between similarity (repetition, alliteration) and the difference inherent in the particular theme that distinguishes each family of sentences. As Beckett reveals in the key, the ten sentences of each section are "'signed' by certain elements common to them all." The signature of Section A, for example, is "true refuge." This phrase appears in each sentence, though its position is not fixed. It is found once at the beginning of a sentence, once at the end, and at different points in between in the remaining sentences. Were all ten sentences to be read consecutively, however, the effect would be less harmonious than balancing the phrase against some quite different image in another group of sentences, such as the "little body" in Section C. The shuffling of sentences, in other words, though arbitrary, has the definite function of balancing a text which, when read consecutively, is overrepetitious. If all the like sentences come together, the balance is lost.

Notes

1. I am indebted to Samuel Beckett and Francis Warner for permission to quote from MSS in Francis Warner's possession; the draft material for *Sans/Lessness* can also be seen in the Beinecke Rare Book and Manuscript Library, Yale University, whose assistance I gratefully acknowledge.
2. Ruby Cohn, *Back to Beckett* (Princeton: Princeton Univ. Press, 1973), 265.
3. Samuel Beckett, *All That Fall* (London: Faber, 1965), 29.
4. See Appendix I. [Not included in excerpt]

5. Samuel Beckett, "Dante . . . Bruno . Vico . . Joyce," *Disjecta*, ed. Ruby Cohn (London, 1983), 27.
6. Cohn, *Back to Beckett*, 263.

Eric P. Levy

The first quality apt to strike readers of *Company*, the recently published work of Beckett's old age, is the strong autobiographical tone. Several of the recollections in the text correspond with incidents cited in Deirdre Bair's biography of Beckett. Perhaps the most remarkable of these concerns an enraged child hurling himself from the top of a huge evergreen onto the boughs below.[1] Yet, to point to autobiography, without recognizing how Beckett's art transforms the very notion of life which autobiography takes for granted, is to imperil the task of interpretation. Let us go back a few steps to see why.

Autobiography is the recounting of one's life as a series of personal experiences or acts occurring through time, lifetime. Strictly speaking, the autobiographical perspective is linear, extending from point B in the present a line of experiences belonging to the same self and stretching all the way back to point A, birth. As a mode of self-knowledge, autobiography is based on extension. That line segment AB, that life, defines the identity of the self located at B; his identity is reflected in his life. Then what kind of identity is this? Fundamentally, it is an identity through exteriority. Life gives intelligible form to all the inner forces and conflicts inhabiting the individual. It tells us what they signified by showing what kind of patterns they provoked or enabled.

It is important to recognize that this linear model is completely antithetical to Beckett's own artistic convictions. In *Proust*, a work of his youth, Beckett contrived the manifesto of his own art in phrases which will help us considerably: "The only research is excavatory, immersive, a contraction of the spirit, a descent."[2] Instead of extension, Beckett invokes contraction; instead of exteriority, a descent towards an interiority too fundamental to be lived—too profound, that is, to be re-

From "'Company': The Mirror of Beckettian Mimesis," *Journal of Beckett Studies* 8 (1982); 95–104. Reprinted by permission of the *Journal of Beckett Studies*.

flected in the line segment called life and the superficial personal identity it traces. This is perhaps the single most important truth to grasp about Beckett's art. He steps beyond the great mimetic tradition of representing reality in terms of life and instead expresses human experience on a level far below the relation of self and world that the linear notion of life assumes. But his art faces a tremendous challenge: how can it overcome the habits of mimesis—"this ballsaching poppycock about life and death," as Malone calls it[3]—and express human experience in a different way?

In the first place, as far as geometric imagery in Beckett's work is concerned, that line segment AB is everywhere bent into a circle, a cycle: the revolving spools of Krapp, the orbits of *The lost ones*, the peregrinations of Molloy, the migration in *How it is*. Beckett transforms the line of life into a circle in order to isolate the centre and excavate it. To ensure that the assumptions of life do not leak into the excavation site, he deploys a complex strategy. As every reader has noted, Beckett creates a prose fiction that insists on its fictionality. Again and again, we hear disclaimers: "It was not midnight. It was not raining," writes Moran,[4] "more lies," says *The unnamable*,[5] "All balls," pants Bom.[6] In *Company*, as we shall see, a figure is lying on his back in the dark, with the ambiguity of "lying" increasingly emphasized. The point, however, is not just that fiction is, after all, merely fiction and not truth, but more significantly that fiction as mimesis is burdened with the representation of a life which in turn is only a fiction, a false or, at best, partial reflection of human identity. Therefore, to neutralize the expectation that fiction represent life or, more precisely, that the experience presented be construed as a life, Beckett, especially since *Mercier and Camier*, foregrounds the very act of imagination creating the fiction. The opening words of *Company* will illustrate: "A voice comes to one in the dark. Imagine."

By emphasizing the act of imagination, Beckettian narration becomes self-referential, a closed system where experience can be presented that relates only to the special purposes of the "reason-ridden" (p. 45) imagination which conceives it and not to the movement of a self through time called life. In the closed system, imagination is free to express experience in alternative modes that resist the reader's tendency to assimilate them to his more familiar notions. Parts of *The unnamable*, for example, present experience as if before birth: "I alone am immortal, what can you expect. I can't get born,"[7] or again, "I shall never get born, having failed to be conceived."[8] *Texts for nothing* suggests a species of after-life or damnation: "I am dead, but I never lived,"[9] as of course do sections of *The unnamable*: "this hell of stories."[10] *Company*, as we shall see, intimates sepulchral existence. These alternative modes, working as metaphors, signify far more about the experience of being human than would be possible on the level of life. Life, with the guarantees of order and meaning we usually take for granted, is explicitly denied, as in *From an abandoned work*: "there never was anything, never can be, life and death, all nothing, that kind of thing, only a voice dreaming and droning all around."[11] Or the negation in *Company*: "No life" (p. 26).

Now let us examine how the excavation proceeds in *Company*. The title, referring to the paradoxical project of improvising company only to deepen the isolation which that company is meant to alleviate, appears in several earlier works. The narrator in *Texts for nothing* says, "Yes, to the end, always muttering, to lull me and keep me company,"[12] while Bom in *How it is* admits, "I have had company mine because it amuses me."[13] *Company* renews this project with astonishing results. The ultimate task of imagination in this text is to express an experience of isolation and interiority so absolute that no company, real or fantastic, can ever relieve it. This is accomplished through the fable of a mirror which contains a reflection or image but which has no model or subject outside to reflect. In other words, the image in the mirror is a *pure* reflection, with no external referent whatsoever. The construction of the fable involves tremendous problems. The story cannot simply present a magical mirror hanging on a wall somewhere and containing an unfortunately stranded reflection, because in that case there would be something—namely the wall, the room, the world—outside the mirror, and these externals would modify the reflection inside by entraining the mimetic expectations Beckett wants to avoid. If the mirror in *Company* is to escape these difficulties, it must occupy the entire text; the entire text, that is, must become the representation of a mirror which has nothing inside it but the pure reflection and nothing outside but the act of imagination creating that reflection.

The construction of this mirror involves three steps. Step I: A body lying supine in the dark hears a voice speaking of the past in the second person, as for example: "You first saw the light in the room you were most likely conceived in" (p. 15). The body cannot confirm that the voice is addressing him and not another and similarly cannot claim the memories as his own. This connection between voice and supine body is in turn the creation of another supine body lying in the dark imagining. The text makes it clear that this act of imagination is, in fact, creating a mirror in which the supine body referred to as "the hearer M" (p. 59) is a reflection of the other supine body named W. Mirror relations between the two bodies abound. Just as the left hand of my reflection arises when I raise my right hand, so the relation of W to M displays the reversal or inversion characteristic of that between model and reflected image. The letter W, of course, is an inversion of M, and repeatedly a movement of the body W is reflected in a reverse movement of the body M, as when W closes his eyes to imagine what M sees on opening his.

Step II: It is now revealed that the act of imagination responsible for creating the mirror does not originate with W, for W is himself created by another "deviser" (p. 34) whom the text insinuates: "Yet another then. Of whom nothing. Devising figments to temper his nothingness. Quick leave him" (p. 64). Later, an infinite series of devisers is implied: "Yet another still? Devising it all for company" (p. 84). The mirror has thus expanded to include the entire text: on one side is the projecting imagination, the inaccessible deviser, with its own voice; on the other, the voice addressing M inside the mirror. The catoptric principle of reversal noted in reference to M and W, applies to the oscillation of style in the text as a whole. The voice in the mirror addresses M in an *earnest* tone. For example, the phrase "you have never forgotten" is attached to many of the recitations to invest them with urgency and validity. In contrast, the voice outside the mirror speaks in the opposite tone of *sarcasm*, implying that all is false, all lies. Some of the hallmarks are a ridiculing alliteration and repetition ("Can the crawling creator crawling in the same create dark as his creature create while crawling?"—p. 73) and ludicrous interjections that undermine the project they are meant to advance. Consider, for example, this preposterous *fiat*: "Let there be a fly. What an addition to company that would be!" (p. 38). Finally, the principle of reversal applies even to the act of imagination considered as an act—that is, as the projecting or tending of an agent toward an end. Outside the mirror, the project is to create company; but inside the mirror that project is fulfilled through the pure reflection—a state of absolute isolation, interiority without identity. Interestingly, the word "company," which appears frequently in the text, is uttered only by the sarcastic voice.

Step III: This last development is, in fact, comprised of several smaller ones. Near the end of the text, the second person voice explodes the fable of the mirrors by naming the reflection, "you," as the devising source: "Supine you now resume your fable where the act of lying cut it short" (p. 87). This recognition does not so much shatter the mirror as reverse it. Where earlier "you" was the pure reflection inside the mirror, now "you" is the model outside the mirror which the infinite regress of devisers reflects. But the change does not bring "you" any closer to a sense of identity, because the infinite regress reflecting him can have, by definition, no ultimate subject. In effect, what has happened is that the pure reflection—that is, the reflection of a self who is not there—now occupies both sides of the mirror.

Next, the last phrases isolate "you" even from the company of the reflected devisers:

> But with face upturned for good labour in vain at your fable. Till finally you hear how words are coming to an end. With every inane word a little nearer to the last. And how the fable too. The fable of one fabling with you in the dark. And how better in the end labour lost and silence. And you as you always were.
> Alone.

The word, "alone" receives tremendous emphasis. In the text, it appears several lines below all the others. But who is alone? That is the question which cannot be answered in conventional terms by pointing to a definite self. The aloneness can be predicated if only one subject—the pure reflection. The text provides no other referent whatsoever. Hence, the project of imagination to make the text a mirror of the pure reflection has been fulfilled and the book can close.

Notes

1. See Deirdre Bair, *Samuel Beckett: a Biography*, New York, Harcourt, Brace, Jovanovich, 1978, p. 15. See also Samuel Beckett, *Company*, London, John Calder, 1980, p. 28. Future references to *Company* will be included in the text with the appropriate page number(s) in parentheses.

2. Samuel Beckett, *Proust and three dialogues with Georges Duthuit*, London, John Calder, 1965, p. 65.

3. *Three novels: Molloy; Malone Dies; The unnamable*, trans. Samuel Beckett and Patrick Bowles, New York, Grove Press, 1965, p. 225.

4. *Three novels*, p. 176.

5. *Three novels*, p. 414.

6. *How it is*, trans. Samuel Beckett, New York, Grove Press, 1964, p. 145.

7. *Three novels*, p. 383.

8. *Three novels*, p. 353.

9. *Stories and texts for nothing*, trans. Samuel Beckett, New York, Grove Press, 1967, p. 130.

10. *Three novels*, p. 380.

11. *From an abandoned work* in *First love and other shorts*, trans. Samuel Beckett, New York, Grove Press, 1974, p. 49.

12. *Texts for nothing*, p. 78.

13. *How it is*, p. 31.

Michael O'Brien

Ford Madox Ford thought that a poem should be written at least as well as prose. Which seems modest enough, until you look at *Ill Seen Ill Said*. How many poems are written as well as this prose? As careful of cadence, as directive in syntax, as delimiting, as conscious, as resourceful, as urgent? It makes for a curious elation. . . . *Ill Seen Ill Said* plays against the grain of prose, of most prose, poor beast of burden. "From where she lies she sees Venus rise" is how it begins. Then we are hurried past by the first of a series of imperatives: "On." Later there will be "Careful," and, surprisingly, "Gently gently." So Lear speaks to himself. This is not a matter of allusion: thus we all speak to ourselves when what we want is for the mind to hold. To hold and to continue, remembering and imagining. That this purgatorial work should remind us of Dante's and Yeats's purgatories is not a matter of larding the goose: it is true to a sense that we do remember until we are shut of it, until we no longer have to. Until then we are "Changed but not enough. Strangers but not enough. To all the ill seen ill said." It is as if it is the remembering and imagining that will end by making us strangers to what we remember and imagine: and then we can go.

In his account of his meetings with Beckett, E. M. Cioran writes:

> About five years ago, we met by chance on rue Guynemer, he asked if I were working, and I told him that I had lost my taste for work,

From "A Note on *Ill Seen Ill Said*," *Review of Contemporary Fiction* 7 (1987): 35–39. Reprinted by permission of *Review of Contemporary Fiction*.

that I didn't see the necessity of bestirring myself, of "producing,"
that writing was an ordeal for me. . . . He seemed astonished by
this, and I myself was even more astonished when, precisely in reference to writing, he spoke of *joy*. Did he really use that word? Yes,
I am sure of it.

It is hard to talk of gratitude and joy faced with these pages. Beckett's
rubric for this work is *strangury*: a painful discharge of urine, drop by
drop. His obsessed prose imagines a death, returns to it again and
again. Though it is not just imagination:

> If only she could be pure figment. Unalloyed. This old so dying
> woman. So dead. In the madhouse of the skull and nowhere else.
> Where no more precautions to be taken. No precautions possible.
> Cooped up there with the rest. Hovel and stones. The lot. And the
> eye. How simple all then. If only all could be pure figment. Neither
> be nor been nor by any shift to be.

Yet in another sense what can it be but imagined? Have we died,
that we can remember our deaths? We imagine how it is for another:
for an old woman: "No shock were she already dead. As of course she
is." But detained a bit, by imagination and memory, "Till all recalled."
There is a rage to be finished in these pages, the blessed word of whose
forced utterance is *less*: "With what one word convey its change? Careful. Less. Ah the sweet one word. Less. It is less. The same but less."
Where is the elation in this? There is a passage in Pascal ("j'ai décou-
vert que tout le malheur des hommes vient d'une seule chose, qui est
de ne savoir pas demeurer en repos, dans une chambre"), one where
it is hard to tell the reprieve from the sentence; I think Beckett re-
sponded to it in *More Pricks than Kicks*: "Was it not from sitting still
among his ideas, other people's ideas, that he had come away?" There
remains an urgency that no idea will still, not even that of absence. So
this furious writing remains non-partisan, engaged only in its own action. Among things that retain their opacity. What is the spur to this?
The imperative? "So on. Till no more trace. On earth's face. Instead
of always the same place. Slaving away forever in the same place. At
this and that trace." This rhyming insistent as Kilroy, as unfree.

At a show last fall Mark Rothko's late paintings seemed things in
nature. For all their art. And for all our sense of Beckett arranging *this*
show, these paragraphs seem like things in nature.

Part 3

Louis Zukofsky has a poem in *Anew* that goes

> The lines of this new song are nothing
> But a tune making the nothing full
> Stonelike become more hard than silent
> The tune's image holding in the line.

This song that is only its own singing is not the same as Beckett's burdened prose. But I invoke it here to point to something; something Jacques Rivette points to when he speaks of "the secret form which is the goal of every work of art"; and I do this not not to make Beckett an aesthetic, the dandy of nausea, but to point to an entelechy: the realization of that which is a thing is by virtue of its form. That activity. From which this prose emerges. We delight in the exercise of such power. This is the source of that elation.

Chronology

1906   Samuel Barclay Beckett born 13 April, in Foxrock, a suburb of Dublin, the second son of William Beckett and Mary Roe Beckett. He later insists on clear memories of "fetal existence."

1920   Preceded by his older brother, Frank (and by Oscar Wilde), attends Portora Royal School, in Enniskillen, County Fermanagh, Northern Ireland, where he excels in sports and bridge.

1923   After passing Exhibition examinations required of new students with mediocre prior records, enters Trinity College, Dublin. Sports, except for cricket, give way to modern languages, especially French and Italian.

1928   Having obtained a B.A. with distinguished marks, opens a promising academic career by teaching one term at Campbell College, Belfast, before beginning a two-year exchange fellowship at the Ecole normale superieure in Paris. Develops a lasting friendship with Thomas McGreevy; also meets James Joyce.

1929   "Dante . . . Bruno . Vico . . Joyce" is published in *transition*, along with the same author's first fiction, "Assumption."

1930   His poem *Whoroscope* wins first prize in a contest sponsored by Nancy Cunard for a poem about time. With Alfred Peron, translates the "Anna Livia Plurabelle" section of Joyce's *Work in Progress* into French. Returns to Dublin in the fall as assistant in French at Trinity.

1931   *Proust* is published. Turns away from academic life, resigning his Trinity position just as his M.A. is awarded.

1932   Returning to Paris after traveling in Germany, translates surrealist poems and begins work on the still unpublished *Dream of Fair to Middling Women*.

1933   Father dies. Begins a three-year residence in London, remembered later as "bad in every way."

1934   *More Pricks than Kicks* is published; also "A Case in a Thousand" and several reviews.

1935   *Echo's Bones* is published.

1938   *Murphy* is published after 42 publishers have rejected it. Having returned to Paris, is stabbed in the street by a pimp, only to be rescued by passerby Suzanne Deschevaux-Dumesnil, a pianist. They soon begin living together and in 1961 marry, though only for testamentary reasons.

1940   Joins French Resistance group in occupied Paris, translating and microphotographing intelligence data concerning German supply lines and troop movements.

1942   Narrowly escapes capture by Nazis, flees with Suzanne to Vichy France, where they remain until 1945.

1945   Following Armistice, visits Dublin, then serves with Irish Red Cross in devastated St. Lô before resettling in Paris. Receives Croix de Guerre and Medaille de la Resistance for wartime service.

1946   Writes "The End," "The Expelled," "First Love," "The Calmative," and *Mercier and Camier* in French. The beginning of a four-year period of sustained writing that produces his most famous work.

1951   *Molloy* and *Malone Dies* are published in French.

1952   *Waiting for Godot* is published in French.

1953   *Waiting for Godot* is produced in Paris. *The Unnamable* is published in French. *Watt* is published in English.

1954   *Waiting for Godot* is published in English translation.

1955   *Texts for Nothing* is published in French.

1956   *From an Abandoned Work* is published in English.

1957   *Endgame* is produced (in French) in London.

1958   *Krapp's Last Tape* is published in English and performed.

1959   Receives an honorary doctorate from Trinity College.

1961   *Happy Days* is published and performed. Shares the International Publishers' Prize with Jorge Luis Borges.

1965   *Imagination Dead Imagine* is published in original French and English translation.

1967   *Enough, Ping,* and *Stories and Texts for Nothing* are published in English translation.

1969   Awarded the Nobel Prize in literature but opts not to go to Stockholm for the award festivities.

1970   *Lessness* is published in English translation. *First Love,* written in 1946, is finally published in the original French.

1972   *The Lost Ones* is published in English translation. *Not I* is produced.

1974   *First Love* is published in English translation.

1976   *Fizzles,* written mostly in French but partly in English, is published in both languages. *All Strange Away* is published in English.

1980   *Company* is published.

1981   *Ill Seen Ill Said* is published in original French and English translation.

1983   *Worstward Ho* is published in English.

1989   Beckett dies in Paris, 23 December.

Selected Bibliography

Primary Works

Collected Short Fiction

All Strange Away. In *Rockaby and Other Short Pieces.* First published by Gotham Book Mart, New York, 1976.

Company. New York: Grove Press, 1980.

Enough. In *Six Residua, No's Knife,* and *First Love and Other Shorts.* First published as *Assez* by Les Éditions de Minuit, Paris, 1966.

"First Love." In *First Love and Other Shorts.* First published as *Premier Amour* by Les Éditions de Minuit, Paris, 1970.

First Love and Other Shorts. New York: Grove Press, 1974. Contains "First Love," *From an Abandoned Work, Enough, Imagination Dead Imagine,* and *Ping,* plus the short plays *Not I* and *Breath.*

Fizzles. New York: Grove Press, 1976. Contains eight "Fizzles," all but one ("Still," number seven) originally written in French. Two others have titles in addition to numbers: number three is "Afar a Bird," and number eight is "For To End yet Again." This last comes first in the French edition (Paris: Les Éditions de Minuit, 1976), and gives its title to the whole (*Pour finir encore et autre foirades*).

From an Abandoned Work. In *Six Residua, No's Knife,* and *First Love and Other Shorts.* First published in *Trinity News,* Dublin, 1956.

Ill Seen Ill Said. New York: Grove Press, 1981. First published as *Mal vu mal dit* by Les Éditions de Minuit, Paris, 1981.

Imagination Dead Imagine. In *Six Residua* and *First Love and Other Shorts.* First published as *Imagination morte imaginez* by Les Éditions de Minuit, Paris, 1965.

Lessness. In *Six Residua.* First published as *Sans* by Les Éditions de Minuit, Paris, 1969.

The Lost Ones. New York: Grove Press, 1972. First published as *Le Dépeupleur* by Les Éditions de Minuit, Paris, 1971. Also in *Six Residua.*

More Pricks than Kicks. New York: Grove Press, 1972. First published by Chatto & Windus, London, 1934. Contains "Dante and the Lobster," "Fingal," "Ding-Dong," "A Wet Night," "Love and Lethe," "Walking Out," "What a Misfortune," "The Smeraldina's Billet Doux," "Yellow," and "Draff."

No's Knife. London: Calder and Boyars, 1967. Contains "The Expelled," "The Calmative," "The End," all thirteen *Texts for Nothing,* "From an Abandoned Work," "Enough," and "Ping."

Ping. In *Six Residua, No's Knife,* and *First Love and Other Shorts.* First published as *Bing* by Les Éditions de Minuit, Paris, 1966.

Rockaby and Other Short Pieces. New York: Grove Press, 1981. Contains "All Strange Away" and three short dramatic pieces (*Rockaby, Ohio Impromptu,* and *A Piece of Monologue*).

Six Residua. London: John Calder, 1978. Contains *From an Abandoned Work, Enough, Imagination Dead Imagine, Ping, Lessness,* and *The Lost Ones.*

Stories and Texts for Nothing. New York: Grove Press, 1967. First published as *Nouvelles et Textes pour rien* by Les Éditions de Minuit, Paris, 1955. The "stories" are "The Expelled," "The Calmative," and "The End." There are thirteen "texts." Also in *No's Knife.*

Worstward Ho. New York: Grove Press, 1983.

Uncollected Short Fiction

"A Case in a Thousand." *The Bookman* 86 (1934): 241–42.

"Assumption." *transition* 16–17 (1929): 268–71.

Plays

Act Without Words I. In *Endgame, Followed by Act Without Words,* and *Krapp's Last Tape and Other Dramatic Pieces.* First published as *Acte sans paroles* by Les Éditions de Minuit, Paris, 1957.

Act Without Words II. In *Krapp's Last Tape and Other Dramatic Pieces.* First published as *Acte sans paroles II* in *Dramatische Dichtungen* by Suhrkamp Verlag, Frankfort, 1963.

All That Fall. New York: Grove Press, 1957. In *Krapp's Last Tape and Other Dramatic Pieces.*

Breath. Gambit 4 (1969): 5–9. In *First Love and Other Shorts.*

Cascando and Other Short Dramatic Pieces. New York: Grove Press, 1967. Contains *Cascando, Words and Music, Eh Joe, Play, Come and Go,* and *Film.*

Catastrophe. New Yorker 10 January 1983, 26–27. In *Three Plays by Samuel Beckett.* First published as *Solo suivi de catastrophe* by Les Éditions de Minuit, Paris, 1982.

Collected Shorter Plays of Samuel Beckett. New York: Grove Press, 1984. Contains all the plays except *Endgame, Happy Days,* and *Waiting for Godot.*

Come and Go. London: Calder and Boyars, 1967. In *Cascando and Other Short Dramatic Pieces.*

Eh Joe. Eh Joe and Other Writings. London: Faber and Faber, 1967. In *Cascando and Other Short Dramatic Pieces.*

Selected Bibliography

Embers. Evergreen Review 3 (1959): 28–41. In *Krapp's Last Tape and Other Dramatic Pieces.*
Endgame, Followed by Act without Words. New York: Grove Press, 1958. First published as *Fin de partie* by Les Éditions de Minuit, Paris, 1957.
Ends and Odds. New York: Grove Press, 1976. Contains *Not I, That Time, Footfalls, Ghost Trio, Theatre I, Theatre II, Radio I,* and *Radio II.*
Footfalls. In *Ends and Odds.*
Ghost Trio. In *Ends and Odds.*
Happy Days. New York: Grove Press, 1961.
Krapp's Last Tape and Other Dramatic Pieces. New York: Grove Press, 1960. Contains *Krapp's Last Tape, All That Fall, Embers, Act Without Words I, Act Without Words II.*
Not I. London: Faber and Faber, 1973. In *First Love and Other Shorts.*
Ohio Impromptu. In *Rockaby and Other Short Pieces.*
Play. London: Faber and Faber, 1964. In *Cascando and Other Short Dramatic Pieces.*
Radio I. In *Ends and Odds.*
Radio II. In *Ends and Odds.*
Rockaby and Other Short Pieces. New York: Grove Press, 1981. Contains *Rockaby, Ohio Impromptu, A Piece of Monologue,* and the prose *All Strange Away.*
That Time. In *End and Odds.*
Theatre I. In *Ends and Odds.*
Theatre II. In *Ends and Odds.*
Three Plays by Samuel Beckett. New York: Grove Press, 1983. Contains *Ohio Impromptu, Catastrophe,* and *What Where.*
Waiting for Godot. New York: Grove Press, 1954. First published as *En attendant Godot* by Les Éditions de Minuit, Paris, 1952.
What Where. In *Three Plays by Samuel Beckett.*
Words and Music. Evergreen Review 6 (1962): 34–43. In *Cascando and Other Short Dramatic Pieces.*

Novels

How It Is. New York: Grove Press, 1964. First published as *Comment c'est* by Les Éditions de Minuit, Paris, 1961.
Malone Dies. New York: Grove Press, 1956. First published as *Malone meurt* by Les Éditions de Minuit, Paris, 1951. Also appears in *Three Novels.*
Mercier and Camier. New York: Grove Press, 1974. First published as *Mercier et Camier* by Les Éditions de Minuit, Paris, 1970.
Molloy. New York: Grove Press, 1955. First published in French by Les Éditions de Minuit, Paris, 1951. Also appears in *Three Novels.* Patrick Bowles and Beckett collaborated on the English translation.
Murphy. London: Routledge, 1938. Reprinted by Grove Press, New York, 1957.

142

Three Novels. New York: Grove Press, 1965. Contains *Molloy, Malone Dies,* and *The Unnamable.*

The Unnamable. New York: Grove Press, 1958. First published as *L'Innommable* by Les Éditions de Minuit, Paris, 1953. In *Three Novels.*

Watt. Paris: Olympia Press, 1953. Reprinted by Grove Press, New York, 1959.

Criticism

Proust. New York: Grove Press, 1957. First published in London by Chatto & Windus, 1931. Aggressive presentation of the youthful author's aesthetic creed and sense of requisite lifestyle.

Disjecta. Edited by Ruby Cohn. New York: Grove Press, 1984. Reprints reviews and other critical writings, including "Dante . . . Bruno . Vico . . Joyce" and "La peinture des van Velde, ou: le monde et le pantalon."

Secondary Works

Biography

Bair, Deirdre. *Samuel Beckett.* New York: Harcourt Brace, 1978. An infuriating, invaluable book. Filled with clumsy psychoanalysis and needless sneers and often written in a style appropriate to a Hollywood gossip column, this biography is nevertheless important for its combination of scope and detail and for the generous selection from its subject's letters, especially those to Thomas McGreevy.

Criticism

Acheson, James, and Kateryna Arthur, eds. *Beckett's Later Fiction and Drama.* New York: St. Martin's Press, 1987. Includes essays on *Company* by Kateryna Arthur, *Ill Seen Ill Said* by Nicholas Zurbrugg, and *Worstward Ho* by Enoch Brater, and an excellent survey by Rubin Rabinovitz, "The Self Contained: Beckett's Fiction in the 1960s."

Beja, Morris, S. E. Gontarski, and Pierre Astier, eds. *Samuel Beckett: Humanistic Perspectives.* Columbus: Ohio State University Press, 1983. Includes essays on *The Lost Ones* and *Company.*

Ben-Zvi, Linda. *Samuel Beckett.* Boston: Twayne, 1986. Excellent survey of Beckett's whole work. Includes brief discussions of "Assumption" and "A Case in a Thousand" and a good overview of the *Texts for Nothing.*

Brienza, Susan D. *Samuel Beckett's New Worlds.* Norman: University of Oklahoma Press, 1987. Deals specifically with fiction after *The Unnamable.*

Federman, Raymond. *Journey to Chaos: Samuel Beckett's Early Fiction*. Berkeley: University of California Press, 1965. An early, ground-breaking study, still useful for *More Pricks than Kicks* especially.

Friedman, Alan Warren, Charles Rossman, and Dina Sherzer, eds. *Beckett Translating/Translating Beckett*. University Park: Pennsylvania State University Press, 1987. Includes a good study of the relationship between *Company* and *Compagnie* by Brian T. Fitch, and Frederik N. Smith's superb essay on Beckett's use of pastoral tradition, which discusses "Walking Out" and *Ill Seen Ill Said*, among other works.

Gontarksi, S. E., ed. *On Beckett: Essays and Criticism*. New York: Grove Press, 1986. Includes good pieces on *Fizzles* and *The Lost Ones* by John Pilling, *Ill Seen Ill Said* by Marjorie Perloff, and *Worstward Ho* by Dougald McMillan.

Graver, Lawrence, and Raymond Federman, eds. *Samuel Beckett: The Critical Heritage*. London: Routledge & Kegan Paul, 1979.

Harvey, Lawrence. *Samuel Beckett: Poet and Critic*. Princeton, N.J.: Princeton University Press, 1970. Good, close analysis of the criticism and its animating principles.

Knowlson, James, and John Pilling. *Frescoes of the Skull: The Later Prose and Drama of Samuel Beckett*. New York: Grove Press, 1980. Good survey of work after *The Unnamable*.

Rabinovitz, Rubin. *The Development of Samuel Beckett's Fiction*. Urbana: University of Illinois Press, 1984. Excellent study, easily the best work available on *More Pricks than Kicks*. Includes analyses of "Assumption" and "A Case in a Thousand."

Bibliography

Federman, Raymond, and John Fletcher. *Samuel Beckett: His Works and His Critics*. Berkeley: University of California Press, 1970. Enormously helpful pioneering effort, still useful. Includes (as Appendix 2) "Variants in the Works of Samuel Beckett, with Special Reference to *Bing*."

Graver, Lawrence, and Raymond Federman, eds. *Samuel Beckett: The Critical Heritage*. London: Routledge & Kegan Paul, 1979. Includes reviews to 1977.

Mitchell, Breon. "A Beckett Bibliography: New Works 1976–1982," *Modern Fiction Studies* 29 (1983): 131–52.

Index

145

The Author

Robert Cochran is professor of English at the University of Arkansas. His biography of Ozark folklorist Vance Randolph won the American Folklore Society's Elsie Clews Parsons Prize. He has been a Fulbright lecturer in Romania (1985) and Hungary (1986) and a Guggenheim fellow (1988).

The Editor

Gordon Weaver earned his Ph.D. in English and creative writing at the University of Denver, and is currently professor of English at Oklahoma State University. He is the author of several novels, including *Count a Lonely Cadence, Give Him a Stone, Circling Byzantium,* and most recently *The Eight Corners of the World.* His short stories are collected in *The Entombed Man of Thule, Such Waltzing Was Not Easy, Getting Serious, Morality Play, A World Quite Round,* and *Men Who Would Be Good.* Recognition of his fiction includes the St. Lawrence Award for Fiction (1973), two National Endowment for the Arts fellowships (1974 and 1989), and the O. Henry First Prize (1979). He edited *The American Short Story, 1945–1980: A Critical History* and is currently editor of the *Cimarron Review.* Married and the father of three daughters, he lives in Stillwater, Oklahoma.